The Freshwater Angler™

Trout Fishing
IN THE PACIFIC NORTHWEST

Skills & Strategies for Trout Anglers in
**WASHINGTON, OREGON, ALASKA
& BRITISH COLUMBIA**

**GARY LEWIS and
JOHN VAN VLIET**

**Creative Publishing
international**

Minneapolis, Minnesota

GARY LEWIS has been walking forest trails and fishing Pacific Northwest waters for as far back as he can remember. He is a newspaper columnist, a magazine feature writer, and the author of eight books, including "Freshwater Fishing Oregon & Washington"

and is the host of "Fishing Central Oregon the DVD" series. He makes his home in Bend, Oregon.

JOHN VAN VLIET is the author of more than half a dozen books on fly fishing and fly tying, including the best-selling "The Art of Fly Tying." An avid fly angler and fly tier, he has fly fished throughout the world and is a regular contributor to the *New York Times*. He lives in St. Paul, Minnesota.

Creative Publishing
international

Copyright © 2008
Creative Publishing international, Inc.
400 First Avenue North, Suite 300
Minneapolis, MN 55401
1-800-328-3895
www.creativepub.com
All rights reserved

President/CEO: Ken Fund
VP for Sales & Marketing: Kevin Hamric
Publisher: Bryan Trandem
Acquisitions Editor: Barbara Harold
Editor: Jennifer Gehlhar
Production Managers: Laura Hokkanen, Linda Halls

Creative Director: Michele Lanci-Altomare
Senior Design Managers: Brad Springer, Jon Simpson
Design Manager: James Kegley
Book Design: Emily Brackett
Cover Design and page layout: Lois Stanfield
Illustrators: Maynard Reece, Jon Q. Wright
Photo Directors: Joseph Cella, Ben Streitz
Principal Photographer: William Lindner
Contributing Photographers: Joel Arrington; Frank Balthis; Hiliary Bates; Erwin and Peggy Bauer; Randy Binder/Minnesota Department of Natural Resources; Joseph Cella; Bob and Clara Calhoun/Bruce Coleman, Inc.; Mark Emery; Ted Fauceglia; Bob Firth; Jeff Foott; David H. Funk; Calvin Gates; John Goplin; Daniel Halsey; Tracy Holte; Paul Horsted/South Dakota Tourism; David L. Hughes; Spike Knuth/Virginia Department of Game and Inland Fisheries; Mark Macemon; Mark Miller; Jack Olson/Colorado Department of Natural Resources; The Orvis Company, Inc.; Buzz Ramsey; Lynn Rogers; Mark Romanack; Stephen Ross, William Roston; Ron Schara; Dick Sternberg; Ben Streitz; University of Washington Fisheries Institute; Jeffrey Vanuga/OVIS; Yukio Yamada

Library of Congress Cataloging-in-Publication Data
Lewis, Gary, 1967-
Trout fishing in the Pacific Northwest : skills & strategies for trout anglers in Washington, Oregon, Alaska & British Columbia / Gary Lewis and John Van Vliet.
     p. cm. -- (Freshwater angler)
  Includes index.
  Summary: "Variety of techniques for catching trout in rivers and streams, including spinfishing, baitcasting, fly fishing. Detailed how-to photography accompanied by step-by-step instruction. Discussion of specific waters in Washington, Oregon, Alaska & British Columbia. Index"--Provided by publisher.
  ISBN-13: 978-1-58923-410-9 (soft cover)
  ISBN-10: 1-58923-410-3 (soft cover)
  1. Trout fishing--Northwest, Pacific. I. Van Vliet, John.
II. Title.
III. Series.

  SH688.N74L49 2008
  799.17'5709795--dc22

                                        2008007066

Printed in Singapore

10 9 8 7 6 5 4 3 2 1

CONTENTS

FISHING IN OREGON, WASHINGTON, BRITISH COLUMBIA, ALASKA

Tap. Tap-tap-tap. For trout anglers, there's nothing like that first bite on opening morning. It's that thrill of the new season that makes an angler forget the cold and remember why the alarm clock rang so early on a Saturday.

Oregon is famous for the tackle-busting trophies of Klamath Lake and the acrobatic redsides of the Deschutes. Central Oregon has more trout water than one person could fish in a lifetime. Head east to the Wallowas and Blue Mountains or west over the Coast Range to try one of hundreds of lakes and streams along the ocean. Trout fishing in Oregon has something to offer everyone.

Washington is a prime destination for trout anglers from all over the country. From Rocky Ford Creek and the Yakima River on the east side to Lake Washington, right in the heart of Seattle, the Evergreen State also has something to offer every angler.

Well-known for its well-fed rainbows, British Columbia's waters offer big fish and big country for the traveling angler. Bring your fly rod and tempt Kamloops trout with chironomids or troll flashers and a spoon from a cartop canoe.

To many, Alaska is angling's promised land. But in America's largest state, where do you start? There's the Kenai Peninsula with its robust rainbows, or Prince of Wales Island with its multitude of rainbow and cutthroat streams. Or head to Fairbanks for trout and grayling in the Land of the Midnight Sun.

In the first chapter we point you to some of the very best trout fishing in the Pacific Northwest. We've picked destinations within a day's drive of the population centers in each state or province. These are the essential waters, representative of many other places in Oregon, Washington, British Columbia, and Alaska. And we give you techniques unique to each region.

In the following chapter, we show you how to catch stream trout under a wide range of conditions. We start by helping you understand trout behavior. You'll learn how trout detect danger, find food, select cover, and react to changes in weather.

Then, we give you a concise course on selecting stream-fishing equipment, including fly rods, lines and tippets, spinning and baitcasting tackle. We'll show you how to stock your fishing vest and how to tie a tapered leader.

The fly-fishing chapter starts with complete instructions for rigging your tackle properly. Every important fly-fishing tactic is presented using a no-nonsense approach. The basic fly-casting techniques are demonstrated with clear photos that make each step easy to understand. You'll learn the most productive ways to fish dry flies, wet flies, nymphs, streamers, and special-purpose flies.

The spinning and baitcasting chapter details everything from the basic casting, trolling and drift-fishing techniques, as well as jigging, freelining, and plunking. And we even show you how to use flies with spinning tackle.

The chapter on special situations will help you catch trout under challenging conditions. You'll learn the tricks that help experts catch lots of trout in high water or low water, in heavy cover, at night, and even in winter. We also reveal the secrets of catching trophy trout.

Whether you're an experienced angler or you're completely new to fishing, this book will help you catch more trout in the Pacific Northwest.

Good Fishing!

Gary Lewis
John van Vliet

OREGON

For limits of rainbows in Oregon, head to Detroit Lake (shown), east of Salem. No other Oregon lake is stocked with more trout.

For the throngs of fishermen who pursue trout in Oregon, fishing season never ends. No matter where you find yourself—whether it is in the foothills of the Coast Range or the Cascades, in the shadow of northeast Oregon's Wallowas, or within sight of the Steens Mountains—good trout fishing is within an easy drive every day of the year.

Willamette Region

High in the Cascades near the headwaters of the Clackamas River is Olallie Lake, famous for its trophy trout. Snowpack limits access early in the season, but the fishing is good. Hatchery fish average 12 inches (30.5 cm), but the big brood trout make the long drive worthwhile. Olallie produces 8- to 10-pound (3.6 to 4.5 kg) trout.

Henry Hagg Lake, southwest of Hillsboro, provides one of the best early-season opportunities for Portland-area anglers. At full pool, Hagg Lake covers 1,100 acres (445.3 ha). Bring a boat or cast from the bank. Fish it March through June and try it again in late September. The Oregon Department of Fish and Wildlife (ODFW) stocks 60,000 legal rainbow trout each year; they average 10 inches (25 cm), but can grow beyond 5 pounds (2.3 kg).

Detroit Lake receives more attention from ODFW than anywhere else in the state. This 3,000-acre (1214.5 ha) reservoir is home to rainbow trout, landlocked chinook salmon, and kokanee. A small rainbow-pattern Rapala or a little crawdad pattern crankbait can be a good producer. Best bets are around campgrounds and stream inlets. From shore, fish the Santiam, Breitenbush, and French Creek arms.

In Clackamas County, 1,400-acre (566.8 ha) Timothy Lake is extra good in the spring. Brook trout get big, feeding on crayfish and snails. In June the rainbow and cutthroat bite picks up and it is possible to get holdover trout that range to 18 inches (45.7 cm). Fish the mouths of tributaries, smaller arms, and shallow water.

Northwest Region

In the Northwest Region, native cutthroat populations can be found in every watershed. It's not hard to find a place to fish, but a boat or a float tube is going to keep you in the action. Many of these waters are regularly planted with legal trout prior to the April opener and some are open year-round. A few waters receive stocks of larger trout that average 2 pounds (0.9 kg), or surplus steelhead averaging 8 pounds (3.6 kg). Stream fishing for trout opens in May.

Early in the year, the sunlight warms the shallows and sparks insect activity. Here is where the trout go to feed. Target the transitions from shallow to deeper water to take more rainbows.

In Fort Stevens Park, 50-acre (20.2 ha) Coffenbury Lake is regularly stocked with trout and surplus adult steelhead. Fish from a boat or walk the trail around the lake. Several docks provide access. Cast Rooster Tail spinners, or fish Pautzke's salmon eggs beneath a float.

Located 6 miles (9.7 km) south of Florence, 3,100-acre (1255.1 ha) Siltcoos Lake is capable of producing 5-pound (2.3 kg) wild cutthroats and holdover rainbows to 9 pounds (4.1 kg), as well as bass, crappie, and perch.

To reach the best water, a boat is necessary. The tributary mouths are good places to catch trout all season. Wind-drift a nightcrawler or a single salmon egg in the Maple Creek and Fiddle Creek arms, as well as the Kiechle Arm and north of Reed and Booth Islands.

Southwest Region

Diamond Lake was poisoned in late 2006 to kill the invasive chub. The lake was drawn down and commercial fishing nets were used to haul out about a third of the chub. Then ODFW administered rotenone to kill the remaining fish. Diamond's historically productive water has bounced back. Clarity is at more than 40 feet (12.2 m), zooplankton and insect life are healthy, and that means rainbows are putting on girth. In 2007 ODFW stocked 178,000 fish, and the aggressive campaign is expected to continue. Bring your boat and still-fish jar baits, or troll small spoons, plugs, or flies early in the morning and late in the evening.

Good trout fishing in Oregon is within an easy drive every day of the year.

When nearby Diamond Lake is too busy, 415-acre (168 ha) Lemolo Lake is a good bet. The lake is famous for big brown trout, but is also a great place to catch a limit of hatchery rainbows or angle for landlocked chinook and kokanee. If a big brown is your goal, fish early and late in the day, using 6- to 8-inch (15 to 20.3 cm) kokanee colored swimbaits.

Containing 3,500 acres (1417 ha), Lost Creek Reservoir has hatchery rainbows, cutthroats, and browns. Try trolling a Wedding Ring spinner and a worm, a Rooster Tail, a Little Cleo, or a Triple Teazer. Go deeper for a chance at landlocked chinook or kokanee.

Hyatt Lake has 950 surface acres (384.6 ha) and big rainbows. The shallow reservoir grows lots of insects. Trout and hatchery steelhead average 14 to 20 inches (35.6 to 50.8 cm).

Fish Lake in the Rogue River watershed has 440 surface acres (178.1 ha) and an ODFW-enhanced trout population. Trout in the 5- to 8-pound (2.3 to 3.6 kg) range are common. Cabins, camping, boat rentals, and a restaurant make it a great place for families.

Central Region

Talk about trout fishing in Oregon and the chances are you'll be talking about the Deschutes River. This is the most productive water in the state. Insect hatches are reliable and resident rainbows run from 8 inches (20.3 cm) and up to 5 pounds (2.3 kg). Good fishing can be found from the headwaters all the way to the mouth, but the best trout action and access is in the lower river, below Pelton Dam.

Mecca Flat provides access to almost 8 miles (12.8 km) of river bank: ½ mile (0.8 km) upstream from the parking area and over 7 miles (11.3 km) downstream to Trout Creek. Here a mountain bike is a big help to negotiate the old railroad bed called the Upper Trail.

Crater Lake is one of Oregon's most popular tourist attractions, but it receives very little fishing pressure.

Brook trout in the mountains, cutthroats on the west slope, rainbows in big brawling rivers, ferocious brown trout in seemingly placid lakes and bull trout and mackinaw that chow on ten-inch kokanee, there is a lot of trout action to be found in Oregon waters.

Odell Lake holds the state record for lake trout, also known as mackinaw.

The float from Warm Springs to Trout Creek is one of the gentlest sections on the whole river. From put-in 2 miles (3.2 km) above Mecca to the take-out at Trout Creek, you'll find good trout water all the way, and some of the highest concentrations of rainbows per river mile (1.6 km). In this section, there is bank access at Dry Creek on the Reservation side of the river. Here you'll need a tribal permit and possibly a mountain bike to move between the best spots.

The next float is from Trout Creek to Nena or Harpham Flat, about 30 river miles (48.3 km) which includes a frolic through the Class 4 Whitehorse Rapids. For bank anglers, the Trout Creek access is a good bet. There is drive-in access at South Junction and this spot can provide some good fishing, but can also be crowded. From Locked Gate, 8 miles (12.8 km) above Maupin, down to Macks Canyon, you'll find good access, with 35 miles (56.3 km) of gravel road paralleling the river.

The Fall River emerges full-flowing from a spring in a grove of lodgepole pine, south and west of Sunriver in the Deschutes National Forest. Flowing 8 miles (12.8 km) east, it empties into the Deschutes between Sunriver and La Pine. The water flows clear and cold year-round through calm, quiet bends bordered by tall grass and willows. Downstream it runs to riffles, rapids, and waterfalls. Submerged logs and channels in the ridged river bottom give cover to trout, while shallow weedbeds in the calm water upstream provide insect habitat.

This is clear water and requires light line. Cast a floating line with a 9-foot (2.7 m) plus leader and 6x or 7x tippet. Use a heavy stonefly

Lake trout (mackinaw) in Central Oregon's Cultus Lake average 17 inches. Still-fishing tactics are great way to get a lot of action. Want bigger fish? Pull a large plug and tip the hooks with bait.

nymph with your primary pattern, a No. 18 Pheasant Tail, Brassie, or Hare's Ear on a 15- to 20-inch (38.1 to 50.8 cm) trailing dropper.

Midges and tiny mayflies make up the main hatches on the Fall River in late winter and early spring. These flies are best matched with Griffith's Gnats and blue-winged olives size No. 18 to 22.

The trout move around dependent on water temperature. If your spot isn't holding fish, move on until you find them. Fall River above the falls is open year-round. Access to the river is good in the area near the hatchery, and upstream on the National Forest land.

The Metolius River arises full-flowing from a spring. It is not the easiest place to catch a fish, but the pursuit offers its own reward. Towering ponderosa pines lean eastward toward the rising sun. Lightning-charred hulks stand rotting alongside their more fortunate siblings. Toppled timber stretches out into the water, providing cover for rainbows, browns, and bulls.

The upper river is calm and placid with grassy runs, gentle riffles, bend pools, and islands. Casting is easy and fish-holding water is abundant. The best access in this stretch is on the east bank from Allingham Bridge down to Smiling River, Pine Rest, and Gorge Campgrounds. This is a river managed for wild trout: native bull trout, rainbows, brookies, browns, and whitefish.

Streamer fishing is popular for anglers targeting the big bull trout. These fish average 3 to 15 pounds (1.4 to 6.8 kg). Zonkers, lead-eye rabbit hair streamers, and Bunny Leeches can be fished to imitate a forage fish or a piece of decayed kokanee carcass. Use a sink tip line with a 5- to

6-foot (1.5 to 1.8 m) leader to probe the bottom, beneath underwater ledges, submerged logs, and heavy brush cover.

When the U.S. Bureau of Reclamation built the Bowman Dam, creating Prineville Reservoir, a productive year-round fishery was established downstream. In fact, the best fishing on the Crooked River is in these 7 miles (11.3 km) below the dam. The water is off-color, full of silt from the reservoir upstream, but also rich in food.

On a cloudy day, look for a hatch of blue-winged olives or other mayflies at about 2:00 PM. When the adults are on the surface, instead of fishing dries try emerger patterns like the Loop Wing Emerger, CDC Emerger, or Winger Emerger. Prior to the hatch, trout may be feeding on mayfly nymphs. A small Hare's Ear or Pheasant Tail will produce during this period. If there's no dry fly action, go deep and small with a two-fly setup. Try a Bead Head Prince nymph with a smaller Pheasant Tail, Hare's Ear, or Orange Scud on a dropper.

In Jefferson County's Lake Billy Chinook, bull trout grow to an average of 10 pounds (4.5 kg). Every year, fish in the low teens are caught. Oregon's state record bull trout came out of this lake in 1989, a fish that tipped the scales at over 23 pounds (10.4 kg). In the spring, bull trout chase kokanee and smallmouth bass throughout the reservoir. When water temperatures go above 55°F (12.8°C), the bull trout follow the kokes deeper. In the spring, rig with 12-pound (5.4 kg) test and cast large minnow imitations in the transition zones between the shallows and deeper water. Start with an 8-inch (20.3 cm) imitation. There are times when smaller baits work, but the big bulls don't get that way by being picky.

Lake trout (also called mackinaw) are found in some of the coldest, deepest waters in the state. Feeding on kokanee, they can grow to 40 pounds (18 kg) or more in Oregon waters. Odell Lake and Crescent Lake, with good populations of the landlocked salmon, produce the biggest fish. Cultus Lake macks are smaller on the average, but here an angler can catch more of them, running from an average of about 19 inches (48.3 cm) and up to 15 pounds (6.8 kg).

The fish move up and down in the water column on a daily basis. Find the right depth on the fishfinder then troll a Hoochie or a large Flatfish or Kwikfish behind a series of flashers. Bait with a large trailing nightcrawler to add scent.

Paulina Lake, in Deschutes County, has long been famous for its trophy browns. It currently holds the record and it is believed that when the record falls again, it will be at Paulina. This 1,300-acre (526.3 ha) lake shares the caldera of Newberry National Volcanic Monument with East Lake. In both waters, brown trout catches range between 12 and 18 inches (30.5 to 45.7 cm), but it's not uncommon to tangle with a 7- to 10-pound (3.2 to 4.5 kg) trout.

Casting lures from a boat to the shore in early spring and in the fall is an effective method for catching large brown trout and rainbows.

Try a brown Rooster Tail when the sun is low in the sky. Trolling or casting for big brown trout with Rapalas or similar minnow-imitating crankbaits brings success.

Browns can be caught shallow in the early morning and late evening. They are found around steep drop-offs and rock shelves in deeper water. When temperatures drop in the fall, the fish move into shallow water to feed. Fish at this time of year become irritable and will strike out of aggression. Target the weedbeds, the downed timber, and the stumps, but don't overlook areas with gravel bottoms or underwater springs.

South Twin Lake receives heavy stocks of legal size and trophy-class fish all spring and summer. This is one of those places that boots out big brood-stock fish. Try Berkley Power Bait or Gulp! Trout Dough.

Southeast Region

Rainbows of 3 to 5 pounds (1.3 to 2.3 kg) are standard fare for anglers on Upper Klamath Lake and Agency Lake, but those who put their time in on the water will often catch much larger fish. Every year a few anglers boat big rainbows weighing in the high teens. Hunt the edges of islands, and cast to downed timber and boulders when you find them. Explore the mouths of streams where cooler water empties into the lake. Keep casting and moving until you find the fish.

Often overlooked by Oregon anglers, Upper Klamath Lake can produce fast action for hard-fighting rainbows that average 17 to 20 inches. Ten-pound trout are not uncommon in this shallow, food-rich lake.

The Chewaucan River flows northwest out of the Fremont National Forest to the town of Paisley, and then southeast into the Chewaucan Marsh and Abert Lake. It's a clear-running forest stream with slow, shallow pools, swift runs, and waterfalls. Good streamside habitat protects trout and provides insect production. Bring hiking boots instead of waders. Managed for native redband rainbows, the fish average 6 to 10 inches (15 to 25 cm), but there are a surprising number of 14- to 20-inchers (35.6 to 50.8 cm). Early in the year, blue-winged olives make their appearance. Later in the spring watch for the March Brown hatch, and carry a few soft-hackled Gold-Ribbed Hare's Ears, Prince Nymphs, and March Brown Sparkle Duns.

Krumbo Lake is stocked throughout the season. Trout that winter-over grow to 16 inches (40.6 cm) in their second year. Every season the lake produces 20-inch (50.8 cm) and bigger trout. Fly fishing is most popular; float tubers launch at the ramp and fish out from the cove to 15 yards (13.7 m) from the south rocky point. A long weedbed stretches from there, north across the lake. Rainbows stack along the weeds.

Dry fly fishing for uneducated high country brook trout provides great sport in the clear water. The fish see the fly from far beneath the surface, streaking upward, sometimes two at a time to slash at the imitation. Food is especially scarce in the deeper lakes so terrestrials are a bonus for the fish that can spot them.

Northeast Region

The 75-mile (120.7 km) Imnaha River heads in the Eagle Cap Wilderness and empties into the Snake River. Much of the lower river is bordered by private land on both banks, but there is public access; look for the signs. Early in the season fish beadhead nymphs. In August and September bring hopper patterns. Bull trout must be released.

Wallowa Lake is the largest natural lake in northeast Oregon. It is home to lake trout, kokanee, bull trout (must be released), and rainbow trout. Rainbows are the main catch and most anglers pursue them on the southern shoreline. Boat rentals, launch facilities, and ample camping and lodging make this a great destination.

For more intimate waters in the Wallowa Valley, take the kids to one of several ponds stocked with catchable rainbows in the spring. Try Marr Pond in Enterprise, Victor Pond, west of Wallowa, and Wallowa Wildlife Pond for good fishing through the end of June.

Pack your fly tackle when the snow melts in the mountains. Base camp at Wallowa Lake and hike it in to fish Ice Lake, Aneroid, Frances, Hobo, or Prospect Lake for brook trout that haven't seen a hook in nine months or more. The fishing can be fantastic.

For Your Information

The Oregon Department of Fish and Wildlife protects native trout and steelhead. On hatchery fish, staff and volunteers remove the adipose (small fatty fin located between dorsal fin and tail) to help anglers tell the difference between wild and hatchery fish. See the Oregon Sport Fishing Regulations for details. Oregon lists their stocking schedule on its website: www.dfw.state.or.us.

WASHINGTON

Whether your passion is presenting tiny dries to sipping brookies, casting spinners for rainbows, plunking with bait, or trolling plugs for big browns, you'll find the action you're looking for in Washington State.

Rainbows, cutthroats, browns, brooks, mackinaw, bull trout, Dolly Varden, kokanee and Atlantic salmon. Washington has more freshwater angling excitement than one angler could sample in a lifetime.

Eastern Region

The Spokane River was formerly one of the most polluted streams in the state. It still isn't the cleanest, but progress has been made and the fishing is good for both rainbows and brown trout. It may take a little bit of driving through neighborhoods to find it, and a little crashing through the brush, but there is decent trout fishing in downtown Spokane.

Try a spinner or a spoon, but make sure it has a single, barbless hook. Early spring and fall provide the best fishing, but a hot summer day is better spent in the river anyway. Fly anglers should take a selection of sculpin patterns and beadhead nymphs, as well as the standard assortment of dries.

Northeast of the town of Republic, in Ferry County, is Curlew Lake. This 870-acre (352.2 ha) lake is stocked with 250,000 to 300,000 rainbows each year. Most run 10 to 14 inches (25 to 35.6 cm), but there are a lot of bigger fish. Curlew is open year-round and, besides the rainbows, has brook trout, largemouth bass, and tiger muskies. Bank anglers do as well as boaters, as long as they don't mind a little company on the shore. Lodging, camping, groceries, and rental boats are available.

Found on the border of Lincoln and Adams counties, Fourth of July Lake is a popular winter trout fishery near the town of Sprague. It is open from December through March. At 110 acres (44.5 ha), the ice anglers can get enough elbow room.

West Medical Lake, west of Spokane, is rich in aquatic insects. Rainbow trout, triploids, tiger trout, and browns grow fast. Still-fishing with bait works very well, and fly fishers score with nymphs fished close to the bottom. The best fishing is on the west side of the lake. Boat ramps, rental boats, docks, showers, and lodging are available.

There are a lot of Fish Lakes around the Northwest, and they usually come by their names honestly. Spokane County's 47-acre (19 ha) Fish Lake is a top brook trout producer. Here, the brookies average 7 to 14 inches (17.8 to 35.6 cm). Some of the best brook trout fishing is in May and June, but mark this one down for September, as well, when the brown trout bite turns on. For brook trout, use nightcrawlers. For browns, cast a minnow imitation or twitch bait. There's a boat ramp at the county park and a store at the resort. Gas motors are not allowed.

Located on the Colville Indian Reservation, Omak Lake is managed for catch-and-release in the spring, but is open year-round. The lake is famous for big Lahontan cutthroat. At 3,240 acres (1311.7 ha), this is the largest lake in Okanogan County. Seven streams feed Omak Lake, but there is no outlet. It is 300 feet (91.4 m) deep at its deepest. Bait is not allowed. Spoons, spinners, minnow imitations, plugs, and flies are used; remember to pinch down the barb. A tribal fishing permit is required.

Hatchery rainbow tend to move in large schools. You can find them by watching the water before you begin to fish. Look for rising rainbows to give away the best spot. On more intimate water, use polarized glasses and watch for moving shadows against the bottom.

Amber Lake, at 117-acres (47.4 ha), receives an annual stocking of 7,500 rainbows and cutthroat fry, and the fish can put on some size due to restrictions and catch-and-release rules in place for part of the season. Try spoons and spinners early in the season and come armed with a fly rod and mayfly imitations in late spring. No gas motors.

North Central Region

Rocky Ford Creek is one of Washington's best trout streams. Best of all, it's open and fishable year round. The water comes from underground and the consistent temperature is what makes the fishery so reliable. Public access and the best fishing are found in the top reach, near the headwaters. Here, the water is slow and wide, averaging 60 to 80 feet (18.3 to 24.4 m) across, lined with cattails, reeds, and sage. Wading is not allowed.

Blue-winged olives and midges are a staple for winter dry-fly fishing; but when a hatch is on, try emergers and subsurface patterns. When temperatures really drop, the standbys are scuds, chironomids, and leeches. Try a leech pattern when nothing else is working. Vary the retrieve to spark a strike.

Lake Chelan, at 33,100 acres (13,400.8 ha), is Washington's largest natural body of fresh water. It is 50 miles (80.5 km) long, averages a mile (1.6 km) wide and its maximum depth is 1,500 feet (457.2 m). This lake is famous for its mackinaw (lake trout) and holds the current state record—a 35-pounder (15.9 kg). The other major fisheries are for rainbows, kokanee, and landlocked chinook salmon. Chinook salmon, kokanee, mackinaw, rainbow, and cutthroat are stocked each year. The primary feed is freshwater shrimp, but trolling works well for the macks and freshwater kings. Find the right depth on the fishfinder, then troll a large Flatfish or Kwikfish behind a series of flashers. Bait with two large trailing nightcrawlers and sprinkle on a blend of crawfish/anise oil scent. Vary the speed, depth, and retrieve constantly to spark a strike.

Trolling works for kokanee as well, but it takes smaller baits and a little corn tipped on the hook of a Dick Nite spoon or Wedding Ring spinner. Jigging is popular for all species. Try a KastMaster or a similar jigging spoon. Bank anglers do well at the south end of Riverfront Park and at Caravel Resort. Lodging, camping, and all services are available at Lake Chelan.

Washington state's biggest rainbow, a 24.45-pounder (11.11 kg), came from Douglas County's Rufus Woods Reservoir in 1998. This long lake is backed up by Chief Joseph Dam on the Columbia. Troll or cast large minnow imitations, swim baits, and twitch baits. Focus on the rocky points and structure, and around the mouths of coldwater tributaries. There are walleye in these waters as well. Trout may be caught on the standard bottom-walking walleye rig tipped with a whole nightcrawler.

For Lahontan cutthroat, head to Lake Lenore in Grant County. This 5-mile (8 km) long, narrow lake covers 1,670 surface acres (676.1 ha).

Its alkaline water contains trophy cutthroats to 10 pounds (4.5 kg), but they average 2 to 5 pounds (0.9 to 2.3 kg). The best fishing is from March through May (catch-and-release season) and again in the fall. Most anglers use a boat; bank anglers find fish at the south end. Bait is prohibited. Single, barbless hooks are mandatory on all flies and lures. Access is good at several public launch points on the east side of the lake. Lodging and camping is on the north side.

Crab Creek flows west and south to feed into Moses Lake and produces some decent trout fishing in some of its reaches. Focus on the Seep Lake area and above Moses Lake. Watch for rattlesnakes.

Prime time to fish the Lenice chain of lakes (Lenice, Nunnally, and Merry) is early summer. These lakes are part of the lower Crab Creek system. Bring the fly rod. Hatches of damselflies and other insects turn on in late May and June, bringing the rainbow, tiger, and brown trout to the surface. Best bet is to bring a float tube. You'll have to pack it ½ mile (0.8 km) from the trailhead to the water. The trout average 12 to 20 inches (30.5 to 50.8 cm). Lenice has 100 surface acres (40.5 ha), Merry covers 40 acres (16.2 ha), and Nunnally covers 120 acres (48.6 ha). The best brown trout fishing is early in the year and late in the fall.

Covering 28,000 acres (11,336 ha), Potholes Reservoir sees aggressive trout stocking, ensuring a good supply of 10-inch (25 cm) trout by the end of April. One of the main bank-angling destinations is Medicare Beach.

If you like more intimate water, Moses, Banks, Soda, and the other Seep lakes all are beneficiaries of the Washington Department of Fish and Wildlife (WDFW) stocking program. Brown trout and rainbows in Dry Falls Lake are managed with selective regulations for a one-fish limit.

Big streamer patterns are deadly for hungry trout. A big mouse/rat fly worked across the surface is sometimes more than a big rainbow can pass up.

South Central Region

The upper Yakima River draws fly anglers from all over the Northwest, especially in September. Roza Dam divides the best trout fishing from the smallmouth bass water below it. There is a 2-mile (3.2 km) tailwater trout fishery below the dam.

The WDFW calculates a trout population of 500 trout per river mile. Most of the trout are rainbows, but there are cutthroats, browns, brook trout, and whitefish as well. The canyon water is accessed from Interstate 84, and there is a lot of good public water in this stretch. In the spring this water warms first, activating the trout and bugs. Expect Baetis mayflies, small black and brown stoneflies, and Skwala stones in April. In May and June, watch for green drakes, salmonflies, and caddis flies.

Yakima County's 40-acre (16.2 ha) Leech Lake is near US Highway 12 in White Pass. This fly-fishing-only lake is well-stocked with brook trout, averaging 8 to 15 inches (20.3 to 38.1 cm), and fast-growing triploid rainbows. Ice-off is usually in May. There is a campground and a launch for small boats; motors not allowed. Bring mosquito repellent.

Northwest Cascades Region

Seattle's 22,138-acre (8962.8 ha) Lake Washington is one of the most productive trout lakes in the state. It is 20 miles (32.2 km) long and 209 feet (63.7 m) deep at its deepest point. Cutthroats run to an average of 2 pounds (0.9 kg) and bigger. There are rainbows that grow to 20 inches (50.8 cm) and beyond.These big rainbows are considered steelhead, and must be released.

Kirkland's Waverly Park provides good fishing from the dock. Other bank fishing options are at Chism, Houghton Beach, and Logboom parks. If you bring a boat (and you should), try the north side of the Highway 520 bridge or the Interstate 90 bridge. Other trolling hotspots are at the mouths of tributaries, in Mercer Slough, along Rainier Beach, around Mercer Island, and along the beaches of the public parks. Deep-troll spoons like the Little Cleo or Thomas Buoyants, or opt for a diving plug.

King County's Cedar River opens in June for a three-month catch-and-release rainbow and cutthroat fishery. It was closed for several years, but reopened with the opportunity to catch bigger fish. Bring a good selection of wet flies and size your tippets to handle 12- to 18-inch (30.5 to 45.7 cm) trout. The river has a good run of pocket water for a mile (1.6 km) below Landsburg. The Cedar River Trail is open to walk-in or bicycle traffic; Highway 169 provides access on the lower river.

At the north end of Deception Pass, just off Highway 20, is Pass Lake, a 99-acre (40.1 ha) fly-fishing-only lake. Rainbow, cutthroat, and brown trout run from 15 to 25 inches (38.1 to 63.5 cm). Atlantic salmon and triploid trout are available as well. Pass Lake is open year-round, but the best fishing is in the spring or fall. There is a boat launch, but no motors are allowed. Camping is available in Deception State Park.

Trout fishing picks up in May when the water warms and insect activity increases. For year-round fishing, try Rocky Ford Creek, one of Washington's best trout streams.

Lone Lake, in Island County, is a 90-acre (36.4 ha), 15-foot (4.5 m) deep lake on Whidbey Island. Hatchery-legal rainbows and triploids grow fast in this shallow water. The best fishing is in the spring and fall. Bring a selection of chironomid patterns; the limit is one fish, (18 inches, [45.7 cm] or longer). WDFW provides fishing access and a boat launch.

Southwest Region

Cowlitz County's Kress Lake has only 26 surface acres (10.5 ha) of water and a maximum depth of 17 feet (5.2 m), but it boots out a lot of trout. WDFW stocks 20,000 rainbows and brown trout each year. Kress is located north of the town of Kalama. Bring a small boat or fish from the bank.

A pretty trout spot north of Vancouver is 28-acre (11.3 ha) Battle Ground Lake. Surrounded by trees and filling the crater of an extinct volcano, this little lake is very deep and popular with anglers around the area. Fishing is open year-round, with the peak of the activity in April and May. WDFW stocks legal and brood-stock rainbows, triploid rainbows, brown trout, brook trout, and surplus steelhead. Bank anglers can circle the lake on a nice trail. Fallen timber provides shoreside cover for trout. Bring a boat or a float tube for the best action. Pautzke salmon eggs and jar baits are favored by many, but wind-drifting with a nightcrawler can ensure a quick limit and a chance at a trophy.

Plan to fish Clark County's Canyon Creek in June or July. This pretty stream is home to cutthroats and rainbow trout. In its upper reaches it is paralleled by a good gravel road.

Lacamas Lake is a 315-acre (127.5 ha), 65-foot (19.8 m) deep lake, conveniently located near Vancouver for thousands of anglers in search of an early-season limit of trout. Browns and rainbows are planted here each year, and there are a few cutthroat available, as well as lots of warmwater fish. The best trout fishing is in the main lake north of the boat launch. Plenty of bank access pays off for the warmwater anglers, while serious trout anglers generally use a boat.

Lewis County's Mayfield Lake is better known these days for its tiger muskie fishery, but this big Cowlitz River reservoir is also a trout fishing destination. Rainbow and cutthroat trout are the main catch, but there are also landlocked coho on the menu.

One of Lewis County's best trout fisheries is Mineral Lake, a 277-acre (112.2 ha) lake at the town of Mineral. Plan to be somewhere else opening day because of crowds. Mineral is a good bet throughout the season (it closes Sept. 30) and a great place for a trophy. WDFW supports the fishing with huge plants of rainbow fry and legals, triploids, brood trout, tiger trout, and browns. Mineral Lake is wheelchair-accessible, and it has ample bank fishing, ramps, lodging, services, and boats to rent.

Mineral Lake is home of the ten-pound trout. Shown here is a seven-pound, twenty-six-inch long rainbow caught using ultra light gear (6 lb. line) rigged with two yellow Berkely power eggs smothered in Pure Cure Sardine Bait Oil above a slip sinker.

Fishing for trout on the Yakima River. Native and hatchery-reared trout are accessible, in water that is open to the public, within a short drive of even the biggest population centers.

Northwest Peninsula Region

Drive north on US Highway 101 from Hoquiam or go west from Port Angeles to Forks and the Bogachiel River, and its tributary, the Calawah. The banks are busy in the winter when the steelhead are in, and in the fall during the salmon run. The sea-run cutthroat enter the river and good cutthroat fishing can be found between August and October. They feed readily in the stream and can be caught on bait, small spinners, and wet flies. They seek out slow water and are found along high banks, under shoreside brush, or clean backwater beneath floating logs.

One of the most effective lures for cutthroat trout is a ⅛-ounce (3.5 gm) black Rooster Tail fished on 4-pound (1.8 kg) test line. Seek out the slower, deeper water where the fish can rest beneath overhanging branches. Cast right to the edge of the bank or the brush, let the lure sink, twitch it, and start to reel, keeping a slow retrieve yet forcing the blade to turn. Fly anglers have good success employing wet flies and streamers in black, olive, yellow, orange, or red. Let the fly sink for a few seconds before beginning the slow retrieve.

In Jefferson County, near Quilcene, you'll find 37-acre (14.9 ha) Gibbs Lake. Open year-round, Gibbs is planted with rainbows and triploids and it also has cutthroats, largemouth bass, and coho salmon. Gibbs is managed for trout catch-and-release, but you can keep the bass.

North of Port Angeles, Clallam County's 370-acre (149.8 ha) Lake Sutherland is a good choice for cutthroat trout and rainbows. Most fish run in the 8- to 12-inch (20.3 to 30.5 cm) range, but there are bigger fish. Early stocking gets the trout action started in March. Kokanee fishing picks up in the summer.

An assortment of Mineral Lake trout caught using natural bait scents. Evergreen State trout sip tiny mayflies and crush baitfish up to one-third their own size.

BRITISH COLUMBIA

Given five lifetimes to spend on the waters of British Columbia, an angler still would achieve no more than a nodding acquaintance with the province's rich abundance of freshwater trout fishing.

British Columbia is an angler's paradise with waters renowned for rainbows, cutthroats, brown trout, and Dolly Varden. The lakes and streams of Canada's westernmost province come alive when the spring sun warms the water and rise rings dimple the shallows. Ply the rivers of the Vancouver Coast or head inland to battle big Kamloops trout or rainbows on the west slope of the Rockies.

Vancouver Coast & Island Waters

Vancouver Island's Cowichan River is considered one of the best trout streams in British Columbia. Reliable hatches and abundant minnow populations make for well-fed rainbow, cutthroat, and brown trout. Plan to fish the upper river (fly fishing only) in April and early May. The important hatches include the Western March brown mayfly (No. 12 to 16) and a little brown caddis. Keep a selection of No. 10 to 14 olive and gray caddis patterns, golden stoneflies, and smaller stonefly imitations.

Bring baitfish imitations like the Lead Eye Sculpin and stickleback patterns. The Cowichan is also a good steelhead stream. Winter steelhead are in the river from December through April and summer-runs appear in June and July, with the peak in September or October. The Nanaimo, the Elk, the Stamp, the Marble, the Nimpkish, and the Muchalat are also worthy Vancouver Island trout streams.

Some of the best trout lakes are in the south part of the Island. Near Victoria, consider Langford, Prospect, Beaver, and Elk lakes. Dugan, Fuller, and Chemainus lakes are also productive waters. In the Nanaimo area, Timberland and Crystal lakes are good bets. Chironomids (midge larvae) are the main food source and are best matched with a No. 14 to 16 reddish-brown pattern. Fish chironomid patterns on a floating line under a strike indicator. On a breezy day, the wavelet action on the surface will provide all the action necessary. When the wind isn't blowing, retrieve your fly with ½ inch (1.3 cm) pulls, keeping the line taut against a strike. Plan the trip between April and October.

The Powell Forest, on the north coast, has good logging road access to a variety of good trout lakes, including Nanton, Ireland, Inland, Dodd, Khartoum, and Lois lakes. These waters are capable of growing cutthroats to astonishing proportions; 20-inch (50.8 cm) cutts are not uncommon and 30-inchers (76.2 cm) are caught each year by the best anglers. Abundant kokanee and stickleback are the reason why the fish get so big.

Bring a full-sinking line and explore the shorelines with a 4- to 6-foot (1.2 to 1.8 m) leader and a leech, sculpin, or minnow imitation. Expect the best insect hatches in April and May. Chironomids, gray drakes, and small Callibaetis are the most common trout food. In the fall, fish kokanee patterns and stickleback imitations.

Cariboo-Chilcotin Region

With soils rich in mineral content and waters rich in nutrients, the Cariboo-Chilcotin Region is a trout fishing destination for anglers from all over the Pacific Northwest. Anglers come to sample the Horsefly River, the Quesnel River, the Blackwater River, and other streams.

Chilko, Eutsuk, Puntzi, Nimpo, and Anahim are some of the better-known lakes, but part of the allure of this region is the chance to prospect the virtual unknowns. A few lakes are renowned for big trout, while many others have smaller fish and lots of them.

Flowing northeastward from the Ilgachuz Mountains and across the Fraser Plateau, the 174-mile-long (280 km) Blackwater River (a.k.a. West Road River) is a tributary of the Fraser River. The river is floatable by canoe or raft through much of its length. Rainbow trout average 10 to 16 inches (25 to 40.6 cm).

Caddis, mayfly, and stonefly patterns will take trout on the surface, while wet flies and beadhead nymphs produce subsurface action for rainbows and whitefish. The Blackwater's rainbows are also well known for their propensity for eating redside shiners. Streamer anglers take note: Chinook salmon spawn in the Blackwater in the fall, and egg

The fertile trout waters of the Chilcotin Plateau take their richness from mountain springs.

patterns pay off for trout at this time of year. An angler should bring a four-wheel-drive, high-clearance vehicle with a winch.

The Quesnel River flows out of Quesnel Lake in the Cariboo Mountains near the town of Likely, and flows 62.1 miles (100 km) to its confluence with the Fraser. Sockeye, chinook, and coho salmon spawn in this stream, making it that much richer for the trout. A tributary to the Quesnel, the Horsefly, is another good trout stream with trout that can reach 16 inches (40.6 cm) or more.

Several of this region's stillwaters are legendary. Nimpo Lake, south of Anahim, is known for producing big, strong rainbows. The most fishing pressure centers near its three resorts. It has an average depth of nearly 40 feet (12.2 m) and is 80 feet (24.4 m) deep at its deepest point. Its shoreline has a mixture of gravel and weeds, with some grass and willows lining the banks. Ice-out is in May. These days, Nimpo's rainbows average 2 to 3 pounds (0.9 to 1.4 kg).

Puntzi Lake, west of the town of Williams Lake, is 4,216 acres (1706.9 ha) with an average depth of 75 feet (22.9 m). Its bottom is sandy and its shoreline is rocky with some overhanging alders. Ice-out is generally in late April. Wild and hatchery rainbow trout and kokanee are the main catch. The lake has four resorts, a campground, and boat launches. Bait fishing is popular here, but trolling is the main technique for boaters. Fly anglers put their time in on this water as well. The best fishing is from May through October.

British Columbia has some of the most popular fly fishing destinations. For dry-fly action, plan a trip in June or July.

Anahim Lake is 200 miles (321.8 km) west of the town of Williams Lake, and with an average depth of 5 feet (1.5 m) and a maximum depth of 17 feet (5.2 m), this 1,470-acre (595.1 ha) lake is productive water. Ice-off usually occurs in May. There are two resorts on the lake with camping available. Rainbows and char are the main catch; wild rainbows average 14 to 16 inches (35.6 to 40.6 cm) and run to 3 pounds (1.4 kg). Trolling and bait fishing take a lot of trout, but this is a major fly fishing destination. Other lakes worthy of mention in the Williams Lake area include Fletcher Lake, Mons Lake, Willan Lake, and Kloacut Lake.

Thompson-Okanagan Region

Rich in nutrients, the lakes of the interior are famous for growing big trout. One of the favorites is Peterhope, a 287-acre (116 ha) lake with a maximum depth of 108 feet (33 m) and an average depth of 38 feet (11.6 m). The ice comes off in May. The lake is stocked with rainbows, which can reach 5 pounds (2.3 kg) or more. Luxuriant weed growth, lots of shallow water, and sunken islands provide for an abundance of aquatic insects.

The Kamloops-area lakes are rich with freshwater shrimp. Chironomids are another major food source throughout the year. Damselflies, dragonflies, Callibaetis mayflies, and caddis make their appearance in May, June, July, and August. The traveling sedge caddis hatches are legendary. Hihium, Island in the Highland Valley, Knouff,

The Vancouver Coast is known for its steelhead, salmon and runs of sea-run cutthroat, but high mountain lakes give anglers a chance to seek seclusion and trophy trout amidst stunning beauty.

Badger, and Lac des Roches are a few of the best bets for anglers looking to experience the traveling sedge hatch.

When planning a trip to the Kamloops-area lakes, also consider 235-acre (95.1 ha) Glimpse Lake or 30-acre (12.2 ha) Blue Lake. Lundbom, Roche, Tunkwa, and Stump lakes are a few of the other great trout lakes in the area.

Millions of sockeye, chinook, coho, pink salmon, and steelhead return to the Thompson River system each year. Draining more than 20,000 square miles (51,800 sq. km) of mountain and forest, the Thompson is also home to sturgeon, rainbows, Dolly Vardens, and whitefish.

Flowing west from Little Shuswap Lake, the South Thompson River and its tributary, the Adams River, are good trout fishing destinations. In the fall, with sockeye in the river, the rainbows and Dolly Vardens feed on salmon eggs that didn't make it in the gravel. Match this "hatch" with a salmon egg imitation.

Below Kamloops, trout anglers can find good fishing for river rainbows to 3 pounds (1.4 kg) or more. For the best dry fly action, time the trip between May and July. Keep a supply of ant imitations in the fly box.

The Rockies Region

The storied waters of British Columbia's Rockies are the Elk River and the St. Mary's River. There are many other good places to fish, but these two productive streams attract the most anglers from around the West. Good fishing can be found between mid-May and June. Plan to make the trip between July and October for the most reliable water conditions. Wild cutthroat and rainbow make up the bulk of the catch, but native bull trout and introduced brook trout are available as well.

Starting high in the Rocky Mountains, the Elk trends south and west to its confluence with the Kootenay River. Regulations allow for various angling methods. A road and trail system make river access easy. The river is driftable in the upper reaches, but portages will be necessary to clear sweepers, log jams, and beaver dams. Bring felt-soled waders and a wading staff to negotiate the crossing points.

The St. Mary's River heads high in the Purcell Mountains and runs east to its junction with the Kootenay River close to Fort Steele. St. Mary's Lake divides the river into two parts: a clear-running mountain brook above and a classic trout fishing stream with runs, pools, and whitewater below.

Expect trout to range between 10 and 16 inches (25 to 40.6 cm). Stock the fly box with No. 8 to 14 caddis patterns in green, yellow, brown, orange, and black. Mayflies are also important, in No. 12 to 14, in gray, tan, olive, and brown. For stonefly imitations, bring No. 4 to 8 golden stones and smaller patterns.

The Columbia River is rarely considered a trout stream, but in its upper reaches it is very productive trout water. In British Columbia the river is vastly different than the stream that divides the states of Oregon and Washington. Resident rainbows and migratory, up-running fish from below the border make the upper Columbia a worthy destination for the traveling angler.

Prospect downstream from the confluence with the Kootenay all the way to the border. Like any tailwater fishery, the Columbia is prone to water level fluctuations and the attendant effect it has on fishing activity. To understand the fishing, break the river into its component parts: shallow runs over gravel bottoms, back eddies that trap insect life and attract migrating fry, and seams that separate fast currents from slow currents. In slower water, drift chironomid imitations below an indicator. In faster water, fish stonefly imitations, including the larger black stoneflies, golden stones, and assorted green, brown, and gray imitations in smaller sizes.

The trout in this stretch of the river enjoy a varied diet of mayflies as well: hexagenia, green drakes, gray drakes, pale morning duns, mahogany duns, and blue-winged olives. Expect evening caddis hatches

Cutthroat trout provide the main fishery on the west slope of the Rockies. Abundant insect hatches provide trout with needed protein throughout the season and the fish are seldom finicky.

Lakes in and around Kootenay National Park range from several miles in length to small, intimate stillwater trout fisheries. Some are capable of producing 10-pound rainbows, while others are less fertile.

in the spring and summer. Grasshoppers and cicadas are reliable food sources in late summer.

Bring a boat and a good map to navigate between launches and take-out points. This is big water. It would be a good idea to employ a guide to learn the river first.

Other British Columbia Rockies Region streams worthy of note include Goat River, Moyie River, and Bull River. Kootenay Lake, Trout Lake, and Arrow Reservoir are good trout fishing destinations. Whiteswan, Whitetail, and Premier are good choices for stillwater fly fishing.

Northern Region

Drive north from Cache Creek toward the town of Williams Lake and beyond and you enter a fisherman's paradise, with more waters than one angler could sample in a lifetime. Some of these lakes, rivers, and streams are well known in angling literature and others are obscure.

Stuart Lake, north of Vanderhoof, Babine Lake, north of the town of Burns Lake, and Takla Lake on the Continental Divide are three large lakes with runs of sockeye salmon and the big rainbows that feed on their fry. But there is a lot of blue on the road map and many of the lakes closest to the main tourist thoroughfares have been stocked with rainbows.

Fraser Lake and Francois Lake are connected by the Stellako River, a 7-mile (11.3 km) freestone stream that is easily waded. Flowing out of Francois Lake, the first ¼ mile (0.4 km) of stream has flat water and reliable insect hatches. Downstream, the river constricts and gains speed, running through a steeper gradient of classic pools, tailouts, and rapids. Before the Stellako feeds into Fraser Lake, it calms and slows again. The Nature Conservancy owns the land cut by the best fishing water. Follow trails downstream from the bridge at Francois Lake for access or scout out unmarked paths down to the canyon water.

For dry-fly action, plan the trip in June or July. Expect hatches of big golden stoneflies, small green stoneflies, and tan and gray mayflies. The sockeye run begins in September and rainbows to 20 inches (50.8 cm) are vulnerable to a well-drifted egg pattern.

The Babine River is one of the best known of the North's trout streams. The river starts at the outlet of Babine Lake and the top 12 miles (19.3 km) contains some of the best fishing. The 4-mile (6.4 km) stretch below the outlet of the lake is called Rainbow Alley, because the trout are concentrated here. Below Rainbow Alley is Nilkitkwa Lake, a shallow, weedy, stillwater trout fishery. Below the lake is a mile of faster trout water.

The Babine has a run of September sockeye, and the fry emerge in mid-May to meet hungry rainbows that congregate in Rainbow Alley. Golden stoneflies hatch in June and the best hatches seem to show in the fast water below Nilkitkwa Lake. Expect the small green stoneflies and caddis flies next. The Babine is famous for rainbows, but cutthroat trout are available as well. Use egg patterns in September during the sockeye spawn. Before fishing, consult the current B.C. Freshwater Fishing Regulations.

ALASKA

Think Alaska and trout and you think well-fed rainbows that grow large on salmon spawn. And that is the reality, but only part of the reality. Alaska's rainbows are famous, but cutthroat trout, Arctic char, lake trout, Dolly Varden and grayling deserve a trout angler's time and attention. Here is a glimpse of a few of the 49th state's best trout fisheries, from the temperate climes of the southeast, to Lake Iliamna back to Anchorage and north to Fairbanks and beyond.

Thousands of Alaskan trout waters are accessible from the road system, but to reach backcountry waters, a float plane is necessary.

Southwest Region

Lake Iliamna is the largest lake in Alaska, with a surface area of over 1,000 square miles (2590 sq. km). It is not heavily fished; it's just too big for most anglers and the weather is too unpredictable. Instead, angler focus on the tributaries of Lake Iliamna and the Kvichak River system. Located 250 miles (402.3 km) southwest of Anchorage, this watershed is one of Alaska's best trout and salmon fisheries. Grayling, char, and lake trout are also available. Time your trip between July and September; trout fishing is closed in the spring.

Some of the largest trout in Alaska come from these waters. Average size is 20 inches (50.8 cm), with fish reaching 12 to 15 pounds (5.4 to 6.8 kg) or more. Favorite waters include the Copper River, Gibraltar River, Tazimina River, Kvichak River, and Talarik Creek. Fly fishing is very popular on the creeks and smaller rivers. Spinning gear is

During the salmon run, grayling and resident rainbow trout (top) pack on the protein by feeding downstream from spawning salmon like this hook-jawed silver (middle). Fly rodders can capitalize on their gluttony with an egg imitation. In June, before the salmon runs hit the Fairbanks area, the focus is on grayling, pike (lower) and rainbows.

appropriate, and a drift rig with pencil lead and a drifted egg pattern can be deadly when the sockeye are spawning.

Air transportation is available from Anchorage to Iliamna. There are lodges, outfitters, air taxis, and guides for the traveling angler. Much of the land is privately owned.

The Naknek Lake and River system is another world-class rainbow trout and salmon fishery, with big char to 20 pounds (9.1 kg), lake trout to 30 pounds (13.6 kg), and grayling in many waters. Naknek Lake produced a 23-pound (10.4 kg) rainbow in 1991. A guide is recommended to shorten the learning curve.

Nearby, American Creek is representative of some of the best trout fishing. Heading in Hammersly Lake, it winds west and south to feed into Lake Coville. This is a narrow river, not very deep and about a dozen yards wide in most places. The fish average 18 to 28 inches (45.7 to 71.1 cm) and can be spotted and stalked in the shallow water. Tactics call for drifting No. 6 leeches, weighted with split shot and presented with fluorocarbon leader. Beadhead Prince Nymphs and Pheasant Tails will provoke the big rainbows, too. Attractor dry flies like the Stimulator can pay off when the fish are oriented to the surface. When the salmon are in the river, a No. 10 to 12 egg pattern is the ticket.

The Alagnak River (a.k.a. Branch River) system lies north of the Naknek. It is fed from Nonvianuk and Kukaklek lakes. Rainbows to 10 pounds (4.5 kg) are caught in the headwaters (Nonvianuk, Kulik, and Kukaklek rivers and Funnel, Battle, Nanuktuk, and Moraine creeks). The season opens in early June and some of the best fishing is when the salmon are running in September and October. A float trip is the best way to sample the fishing here. Brown bears are often seen along the river.

The Nushagak River hosts runs of all five species of salmon, Arctic grayling, northern pike, char, and lake trout. With all of those species putting eggs in the gravel, the resident rainbow put on a lot of weight, feeding on the spawn and on the abundant fry. The upper Nushagak is accessed by small plane from Dillingham and Iliamna. One of its best trout tributaries is the King Salmon River. Among the Nushagak's main tributaries is the Mulchatna River, and this system drains the water from thousands of square miles of southwest Alaska. The Mulchatna's principal tributaries, the Chilikadrotna, Stuyahok, and Koktuli offer great fishing for well-fed rainbows. Many anglers opt for five- to seven-day float trips in rafts or kayaks.

South Central Region (Anchorage Area)

The Kenai is probably Alaska's best-known river. People travel from all over the world for a chance to battle with sockeye salmon, silvers, or big kings. The richness of this watershed contributes to the health of the rainbow trout population. The Kenai is divided into two parts by Skilak Lake: the upper and lower. Both sections of river contain large rainbows and Dolly Vardens up to 15 pounds (6.8 kg). A drift boat is the best way to access the upper river. No motors are allowed on this stretch.

Good fishing for rainbows can be found in the lower river, in the first few miles (km) below the outlet of Skilak Lake. Other good bets are Moose River, Killey River, Beaver Creek, Funny River, and King County Creek. For stillwater trout, try Kelly, Peterson, or Watson.

Jewel Lake is one of several Anchorage area lakes that are stocked with Arctic char, landlocked salmon, and rainbow trout for the pleasure of local anglers. Located near the south end of town, Jewel has bank access for the boatless and ramps for launching small craft. The fishing is good in May and June and again in the fall.

The Deshka River is in the lower Susitna drainage, 35 miles (56.3 km) northwest of Anchorage. It is one of the premier king salmon rivers in the area, and there are plenty of resident rainbows and grayling to please the traveling angler. Focus on the upper river in late August and on through the fall.

When the water drops in early summer, anglers may see holding trout in the crystal-clear water. Polarized glasses help to cut the glare.

The Talkeetna River, in the Susitna drainage, is another famous salmon stream. For much of the year it runs with a milky tint, but it clears up in the spring and in the fall. Upstream, the angler can find good trout fishing in the main river and in tributaries like Larson Creek, Clear Creek, Disappointment Creek, and Prairie Creek.

The Talachulitna River is a good choice for a float trip. A tributary of the Yentna River, it is located about 60 miles (96.5 km) west of Anchorage. Rainbow trout run 12 to 15 inches (30.5 to 38.1 cm), but there are bigger ones. The middle and upper river offer the best trout and grayling fishing. For access, charter a floatplane to the Judd Lake headwaters or to Hiline Lake, or to the mouth.

Southeast Region

Ohmer Creek is on Mitkof Island, 21 miles (33.8 km) south of Petersburg. Accessible by car from the Mitkof Highway, it is one of several creeks reached by the road system. Salmon fishing is the main attraction, but sea-run cutthroats, steelhead, and Dolly Varden are available.

Accessed by floatplane, Swan Lake is another famous destination in the Petersburg area. Bring a raft and plan to troll or wind-drift. Fish average 12 inches (30.5 cm) and can be sighted in the clear water, but don't plan to be there earlier than the end of June unless you bring an auger to drill through the ice.

Located 45 miles (72.4 km) east of Ketchikan, in the rainforests of the Misty Fjords National Monument Wilderness, you'll find the Wilson River and the Blossom River. Blessed with a good run of silver salmon, these waters also support runs of sea-run cutthroat. For a chance at a trophy trout, head to Wilson Lake, known for producing big cutthroats, including the current state record. Spring and fall offer the best fishing.

Most anglers go to Alaska to fish for salmon, but the trout fishing is world-class and rainbows get big in the protein-rich water.

Humpback Creek, 50 miles (80.5 km) southeast of Ketchikan, turns out excellent fishing for large sea-run cutthroats and Dolly Vardens. The best times are in the spring and in the fall. Humpback Lake, a long and narrow body of water, offers good fishing for resident cutthroats and Dolly Vardens. Access is by floatplane or boat out of Ketchikan.

On the western side of the Misty Fjords National Monument, Manzanita Lake is worth a visit. Access is via floatplane or by boat to the mouth of Manzanita Creek. A trail follows the creek upstream to the lake. Cutthroats, kokanee, and Dolly Vardens are in the lake. The creek supports four runs of salmon and sea-run cutthroat.

West across the strait from Ketchikan lies Prince of Wales (POW) Island, with more water than one person could sample in a lifetime. The rivers with their runs of steelhead and salmon get most of the attention, but there is prime trout fishing to be had in the lakes as well. Look at the map and you'll see a lot of blue on the ground. You'll see why if you visit in May or September. The rain is nearly constant, but it is the rain that makes this a great place to fish.

Some of POW's lakes are accessed from the road system and others are reached by boat or floatplane. The Luck Lake and Eagle Creek system is reached by car on the road from Coffman Cove or Thorne Bay. The fishing for sea-run and resident cutthroats and rainbows is best in the spring.

Klawock River, near the towns of Klawock and Craig, is a short, tea-colored stream with huge runs of salmon, some steelhead, and good numbers of sea-run cutthroat and rainbow trout. Bring spinning gear and cast Rooster Tails, or pack the fly tackle and swing small streamers. Spring is best for the trout and the steelhead.

Plan on sharing POW's fishing with the bears if your trip coincides with the salmon runs. There are no brown bears on Prince of Wales Island, but there are more black bears than almost anywhere else in the world.

The Thorne River is the largest river system on Prince of Wales Island, draining close to thirty lakes and ponds and a lot of real estate through tributary streams. It is accessible by road and by streamside trails.

Wild steelhead and large runs of chums, pinks, and silver salmon make this a great location for angling for the resident rainbows, cutthroats, and Dolly Vardens. Sea-run cutthroats and Dolly Vardens follow the steelhead upriver in the spring and feed on the eggs that don't make it in the gravel. Like the Klawock, the water is stained with tannin and visibility is poor. Flashy minnow imitations, small flies like the Teeny Nymph, and egg patterns are very effective.

Parts of the river are heavily fished due to the easy access. Other parts of the river are remote and see few anglers. Some anglers follow a three-day canoe route on the Thorne that takes them far from the road system.

Central Region (Fairbanks Area)

In the Fairbanks area there are a number of lakes that are stocked with rainbow trout, landlocked silvers and chinooks, grayling, and char. Chena Lake, east of Fairbanks, is one example. Located on Eielson Air Force Base, Chena Lake is popular with local anglers and can be fished year-round. All methods are appropriate here. The Chena River is a great place to fish for wild grayling.

The Arctic grayling is a fish of clean, cold waters and can be found in North America in isolated pockets in the Rocky Mountains, the Yukon, Northwest Territories, and parts of British Columbia, Alberta, and Saskatchewan. In the Yukon-Tanana drainage there are several famous grayling streams, including the upper reaches of the Chena and the Salcha. Many of these waters are wide open for jet boats.

The Salcha River, like many rivers of the north, is always in search of another way. With every ice-out and every flood it sends fingers through the timber to tear new riverbeds from the taiga. Salcha River grayling average 10 to 18 inches (25 to 45.7 cm). These are graceful fish with small silvery-bronze scales and speckles behind the gills, but their most prominent feature is a towering, speckled purple-green-gray dorsal fin.

While it is great fun to hook grayling on any gear, these are primarily insect eaters and are best matched to a 4- or 5-weight fly rod. Best of all, they're not sophisticated. Match the hatch if you'd like, but in most waters grayling will rise to anything from a No. 18 midge to a No. 8 Royal Wulff. The river grayling you'll catch between July and September may be gorged on salmon eggs. If you plan your trip for later in the summer, be sure to bring a supply of Glo Bug single egg patterns or a jar of Pautzke's where legal.

For information on traveling and fishing in the Fairbanks area, visit www.explorefairbanks.com.

In July and August, the best Fairbanks-area trout fishing is found on lakes that are stocked with rainbows and landlocked salmon. Most lakes are seeded with legal-size fish, but a few receive plants of big brood stock rainbows.

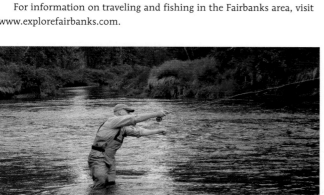

Don Lewis casting for grayling on the Salcha River. Best trout fishing around Fairbanks is in the area's lakes and ponds. On rivers like the Salcha, grayling are the favorite species.

Chapter 1
TROUT & SALMON BASICS

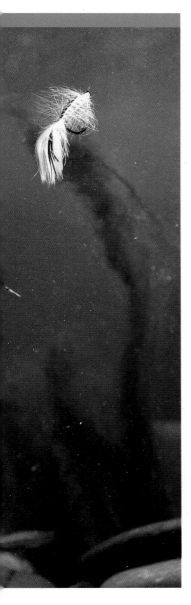

Trout and salmon have long been considered superior gamefish, the ultimate in wariness and fighting ability. In years past, many anglers regarded them as the only true gamefish.

Unfortunately, this wary nature has led to the popular notion that the fish are intelligent, and therefore difficult for the average angler to catch. However, there is no evidence to indicate they are more intelligent than other gamefish species.

The notion of intelligence is reinforced when anglers see feeding trout being "put down" by even the slightest movement or vibration. However, this is an instinctive reaction, and should not be confused with intelligence. Like any other fish, trout flee for cover to avoid predators. As soon as they hatch, trout face attacks from predatory insects, crayfish, and other small fish. As they grow older, trout are attacked by larger fish and by kingfishers, herons, and other predatory birds. A trout's wariness is also the result of natural selection; those that lack sufficient wariness do not live to reproduce.

Their preference for cold water distinguishes trout and salmon from other gamefish. Although temperature preferences vary among trout and salmon species, most seek water temperatures from 50 to 65°F (10 to 18°C), and avoid temperatures above 70°F (21°C). This requirement means they can live only in streams or lakes fed by cold water sources such as springs or snowmelt, or in lakes with deep, unpolluted water.

Trout and salmon belong to the family Salmonidae. Besides trout and salmon, the family includes grayling, found mainly in Alaska, the Yukon, and the Northwest Territories; and whitefish, which are widely distributed in the northern states and Canada but have minor importance to anglers.

For the purposes of this book, the term "trout" includes not only true trout (genus *Oncorhynchus* and *Salmo*) but also chars (genus *Salvelinus*). True trout, such as browns and rainbows, have dark spots on a light background; chars, such as brook trout and Dolly Varden, have light spots on a dark background. Chars require colder water than true trout.

Dark spots on light background: Trout
and Atlantic Salmon

Light spots on dark background: Char

Atlantic salmon are closely related to brown trout and belong to the same genus, *Salmo*. Pacific salmon belong to a different genus, *Oncorhynchus*, meaning "hooknose," and are related to rainbow trout. Pacific salmon spawn only once, dying soon afterward; other members of the family may live to spawn several times. All salmon species are anadromous; they spend their lives at sea, and then return to freshwater streams to spawn. Salmon stocked in freshwater lakes spawn in lake tributaries.

Many species of trout, including rainbow, brook, brown, and cutthroat, have anadromous forms with a different appearance than the forms limited to freshwater. The anadromous forms are generally sleeker and more silvery.

Powerful fighters, trout and salmon have remarkable stamina. Some species, like rainbow trout and Atlantic salmon, leap repeatedly when hooked; others, like brook trout, wage a deep, bulldog-style battle. Most trout and salmon are excellent eating, but there is a strong trend toward catch-and-release fishing. In some heavily fished water, catch-and-release is mandatory. This has long been the accepted practice for Atlantic salmon because the species is so rare and so treasured as a gamefish. Catch-and-release fishing ensures that the fish remain in a stream long enough to spawn and produce "wild" progeny. The other alternative, frowned upon by most trout enthusiasts, is put-and-take stocking of hatchery-reared trout.

To become a successful trout or salmon angler, you must shed the notion that there is an aura of mystery surrounding these fish. Although they live in prettier settings than most other fish, they have the same behavior patterns and the same needs for food and cover. Learn to think of their basic needs and you will have no trouble finding them. Learn to approach them stealthily, like a predator, and you will have no trouble catching them.

Dorsal Fin Adipose Fin Caudal Fin

Gill Cover

Pectoral Fin

Pelvic Fin

Anal Fin

SENSES

Stream fishermen know that a sudden movement, a heavy footstep, a shadow, or a fly rod glinting in sunlight will send a trout scurrying for cover. Salmonids depend mainly on vision to detect danger, but they also have an excellent sense of smell and a well-developed lateral-line sense.

VISION. When approaching salmonids, remember that they can view the outside world clearly through a "window," a circular area on the surface of the water whose size depends on the depth of the fish. The diameter is slightly more than twice as wide as the fish is deep. A trout at a depth of 2 feet (61 cm) would have a window 4 feet, 6 inches (137 cm) wide. Surrounding the window, the surface is a mirror, so the fish can't see out.

Many frustrated fishermen can attest that salmonids have excellent color vision. An olive nymph may produce fish after fish, but a similar nymph in a slightly darker green will not draw a strike. Because the

When approaching salmonids, remember that they can view the outside world clearly through a "window," a circular area on the surface of the water whose size depends on the depth of the fish. The diameter is slightly more than twice as wide as the fish is deep. A trout at a depth of 2 feet (61 cm) would have a window 4 feet, 6 inches (137 cm) wide. Surrounding the window, the surface is a mirror, so the fish can't see out.

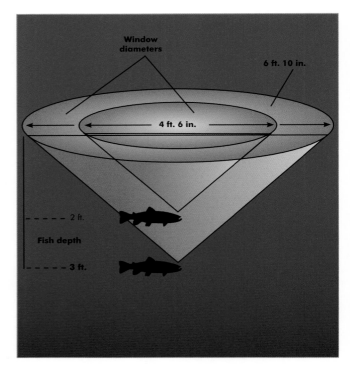

fish are so color selective, experienced anglers often carry similar fly or lure patterns in several different colors or shades in an attempt to determine the color of the day.

Trout and salmon have only fair night vision. With the exception of large brown trout, they do little feeding after dark. Even browns seem to have difficulty locating a fly unless it produces noise or vibration.

SMELL. Trout and salmon use their sense of smell to find food, avoid predators, and locate spawning areas. If you drop a gob of fresh salmon eggs in a clear pond filled with rainbows, the eggs will "milk" as they sink, leaving a scent trail. Feeding trout mill about until they cross the trail, then they turn and follow it to the eggs.

Researchers in British Columbia found that salmon turned back from their spawning run and headed downstream when a bear was fishing upstream of them. The salmon detected a chemical emitted by the bear called L-serine. This chemical is also given off by human skin.

Salmon and migratory forms of trout navigate at sea or in large lakes by using the sun, currents, and the earth's magnetic field. These clues enable them to return to the vicinity of their home stream at spawning

Salmon returning to spawn use their keen sense of smell to detect the presence of bears far upstream.

time. Once they get that far, they rely on scent to find just the right stream. Amazingly, they can return to the exact area of the stream where their lives began. When researchers cut a salmon's olfactory nerves, it could not find its way back.

Biologists have discovered that they can dramatically increase the percentage of chinook salmon returning to a given stream by "imprinting" the young fish before they move to open water. Just as the young start to smolt, a chemical that can be detected in extremely low concentrations is dripped into the stream. The smell of this chemical is somehow locked into the fish's memory. Then, when the salmon reach maturity, the same chemical is again dripped into the stream. In some cases, this technique has doubled the return rate.

LATERAL LINE. Veteran stream fishermen step very lightly when wading the streambed or walking the bank, even when outside the fish's field of vision. They also realize that vibration-producing lures work better in murky water or after dark than lures that produce little vibration. The fish evidently detect footsteps and lure vibrations with their lateral-line system, a network of ultra-sensitive nerve endings along the side of the body.

FEEDING & GROWTH

During their early years, trout and salmon feed mainly on immature forms of aquatic insects, and to a lesser extent on adult insects, both aquatic and terrestrial. They also eat small crustaceans, mollusks, and earthworms. As they grow larger, they continue to eat large numbers of insects, but small fish make up an increasing percentage of their diet. Large trout do not hesitate to eat small animals like frogs and mice. Some salmon species, such as sockeye and pink, are plankton feeders, filtering tiny organisms from the water with their closely spaced gill rakers. This feeding behavior makes them very difficult to catch on hook and line. Practically all trout and salmon will eat the eggs and young of other species, and of their own kind, when the opportunity presents itself.

How fast a trout grows depends not only on the type of food it eats, but also on the fertility and size of the stream.

Generally, trout that feed primarily on insects grow more slowly than those that eat small fish; insect feeding uses more energy for nutrients obtained. Trout in mountain streams usually grow more slowly than trout in farm-country streams. The high altitude streams are colder and less fertile, so they produce considerably less food. Brown trout, for instance, seldom exceed 1 pound (0.45 kg) in small mountain streams where insects are the major food. In contrast, they grow to 15 pounds (7.4 kg) or more in rivers with marginal temperatures for trout but with plenty of baitfish.

Trout that live in small brooks have a slower growth rate than those in good-sized rivers because the bigger water offers a greater abundance and diversity of foods. The size of the spawning stream also seems to affect the size of chinook salmon, even though the salmon do very little feeding in the stream. Studies have revealed that the larger the spawning stream, the larger the salmon.

Genetics also influence growth rate. Fast-growing strains of many species have evolved naturally or have been produced by fish culturists who select and breed the fastest-growing individuals from each year-class. Donaldson rainbow trout, a strain selectively bred for fast growth at the University of Washington, may reach 10 pounds (4.5 kg) in only two years, provided they have enough food. A normal rainbow of the same age weighs less than a pound (0.45 kg), even if food is abundant.

Male trout and salmon grow faster than females; salmonids differ in this respect from most other fish species.

SALMONID DIET & LIFE SPAN

Species	Common Foods	Max. Age in Years
Rainbow trout	Mainly insects; also plankton, fish eggs, small fish, crustaceans	11
Brown trout	Primarily insects; large browns feed mostly on fish and crayfish	8
Cutthroat trout	Mostly insects and small fish; also fish eggs, crustaceans, and frogs	9
Golden trout	Insects, especially caddisfly and midge larvae; also crustaceans	7
Brook trout	Mainly insects and small fish; diet extremely varied	15
Bull trout	Mainly fish; also insects, mollusks, and crustaceans	19
Dolly Varden	Mainly small fish and fish eggs; also insects	19
Arctic char	Small fish, fish eggs, insects, and plankton	40
Arctic grayling	Mainly insects and fish eggs; also small fish, mollusks, and crustaceans	10
Pink salmon	Plankton, crustaceans, squid, and small fish	Normally 2, up to 3
Chinook salmon	Mostly fish; also squid and crustaceans	Normally 4, up to 9
Coho salmon	Mainly fish; also crustaceans	Normally 3, up to 5
Chum salmon	Plankton, small fish, squid, and crustaceans	Normally 4, up to 7
Sockeye salmon	Mostly plankton and small crustaceans; also small fish and bottom organisms	Normally 4, up to 8
Atlantic salmon	Crustaceans, insects, and small fish	14

Common Stream Insects

In the quest to "match the hatch," some fly-fishing enthusiasts spend many hours studying stream insects and tying flies that closely mimic the real thing. Some experts can identify hundreds of different insect species and tie flies to match. However, in most situations, you do not have to duplicate hatching insects so precisely. If you can recognize the insect group, and the life stage of the group that the trout are feeding on, and then use a fly about the same size, shape, and color, you can catch all but the most selective trout.

Stream insects are grouped into four major orders represented by thousands of species. These orders include mayflies, caddisflies, stoneflies, and midges.

MAYFLIES. Among the most common aquatic insects in eastern and midwestern streams, mayflies are especially abundant in limestone streams and spring creeks. They normally have a one-year life span, most of which they spend as a nymph. Mayfly nymphs are easily recognized by the single pair of wing pads, and gills on the upper surface of the abdomen. Most species have three long tail filaments.

When a mayfly nymph matures, it swims to the surface, its skin splits down the back, and a subimago, or dun, emerges. The dun drifts on the surface until its wings dry, and during this time it is an easy target for trout. It then flies to streamside vegetation and after a day or two transforms into a sexually mature adult, or spinner. Duns have grayish or brownish upright wings; spinners have clear upright wings, more vibrant colors, and longer tail filaments. Mayflies are the only aquatic insects with this two-step adult stage.

STAGES OF A MAYFLY

Mayfly nymph (left); mayfly subimago, or dun (middle); mayfly adult, or spinner (right).

STONEFLIES. These insects abound in the West, especially in cold mountain streams. They will not tolerate pollution or warm water, so they make good indicators of water quality.

Like a mayfly, a stonefly spends most of its aquatic life as a nymph. The nymphal stage lasts from one to four years. Stonefly nymphs have two pairs of wing pads instead of one, two short tail filaments instead of three long ones, and the gills are on the underside of the thorax, rather than the upper surface of the abdomen. Adults are dull-colored, with wings that lie flat against the back.

CADDISFLIES. In the majority of trout streams, caddisflies are the most common aquatic insect. They are more tolerant of pollution and warm water than most other aquatic insects. Their life cycle consists of two aquatic stages, the larva and the pupa. The small wormlike larva is cream-colored, with a dark head and three sets of jointed legs near the front of the body. It often lives in a case built from sand grains, twigs, or other debris. The larval cases are commonly attached to rocks. Some larvae roam freely over the bottom, with or without cases. These are the ones most often eaten by trout.

After about a year, the larvae seal themselves into their cases to pupate. These cases are usually attached to a rock or other object. Inside the cases, the pupae develop legs and wing pads. After a few weeks they chew through their cases, crawl out, and dart for the surface. There, they transform quickly into adults and fly away. The adults are grayish or brownish, with tent-like wings.

Overall, caddis larvae are much more important as trout food than the pupae or adults. Although trout will eat pupae in their cases, the pupae are most vulnerable as they swim for the surface.

STAGES OF A CADDISFLY

Caddisly larva with case (left); caddisfly adult (right).

Midge larvae (left); midge adult (right).

MIDGES. This group includes the tiniest aquatic insects. Midges are most numerous in slow-moving, vegetated stream stretches. Like caddisflies, midges have larval and pupal stages.

Midge larvae are more slender than caddis larvae. They do not have jointed legs or live in cases. Normally, the larvae cling to vegetation or bottom debris. Some burrow into mucky bottoms. A trout may consume hundreds of the tiny larvae each day.

After several months the larvae begin to pupate, but some kinds do not form cases to do this. Instead, they move about actively for about two weeks before maturing and swimming to the surface. The legs of adult midges are long, especially the forelegs, and look quite frail. Trout feed heavily on the pupal and adult forms.

One sure way to find out what a trout has been eating is to pump its stomach. But first you have to catch a trout. Even with no trout in hand, you can get an idea of their diet by seining with a fine-mesh net or turning over rocks, then examining the clinging insects.

A hatch chart can give you some guidelines on the type of insect likely to be hatching in your region at a certain time of year and time of day. But hatch charts can be misleading, because different streams in the same region have different hatches, and hatching times can vary by several weeks depending on the weather.

You may be able to get more specific information on hatches in a particular stream by inquiring at a local fly shop.

Understanding the Rise

A rise is the surface disturbance that results when a trout or salmon takes a floating insect. A rise can tell you not only where the fish is located, but also what it is eating. Inexperienced anglers often make the mistake of casting directly to a rise in hopes of catching the trout. However, in most cases, the rise occurs well downstream of the trout's lie. To present your fly where the trout is holding, you must cast well upstream of the rise. By watching exactly how trout are rising, you can get an idea of what type of insect they are taking. You may be able to determine the life stage of the insect, the group it belongs to, and possibly the exact species. This information helps you arrive at a strategy for catching the trout.

HOW A TROUT TAKES A FLOATING INSECT

Feeding trout face into the current. They watch the surface closely to spot insects or other food drifting into their window of vision.

After spotting an insect, a trout drifts downstream tail first while carefully examining the food. The trout may drift only a foot or two (30 to 60 cm), or as much as 25 feet (762 cm).

The trout rises to take the insect, leaving a noticeable ring on the surface. The tendency of most anglers is to cast just upstream of the ring.

Immediately after rising, the trout returns upstream to its lie. If you cast just above the ring, your fly alights too far downstream, behind the trout's window of vision.

SIP RISE. Generally means trout are surface-feeding on mayfly duns or stoneflies. A trout sucks in the insect without breaking the surface. In smooth water you see a wing; in broken water it may not be apparent. Cast a dry mayfly or stonefly imitation well ahead of the rise.

HEAD-AND-TAIL RISE. Usually means the trout is feeding on insects in the surface film. The head appears first; then, as the fish rolls, you see the dorsal fin, and finally the tail. Cast a spinner, terrestrial, nymph, or midge pupa well upstream of the rise and let it drift naturally.

SPLASH. The trout completely clears the water, usually to catch emerging insects such as caddisflies, or insects dipping in the water to deposit eggs. Use a wet fly, angle your cast downstream, then let the current swing the fly to the trout. Or, skate a caddis dry fly on the surface.

TAILING. Technically, this is not a rise because the fish is not feeding on the surface. When you see a protruding tail, the trout is probably rooting immature insects or scuds from the bottom. Drift a nymph or scud pattern along the bottom to the fish.

SPAWNING BEHAVIOR

Salmonid spawning habits vary greatly among species. Most spawn in fall, but some, like the rainbow trout, spawn in spring. Trout, char, grayling, and Atlantic salmon can live to spawn several times. Salmonids require flowing water to spawn, but brook trout and sockeye salmon sometimes spawn in lakes. All but the grayling dig a redd, or nest, for depositing their eggs.

PHYSICAL CHANGES. Before spawning, trout and salmon, particularly the males, undergo astounding anatomical changes. A male's jaws lengthen and the lower jaw develops a large hook, or kype. The teeth of male Pacific salmon grow much larger before spawning, evidently to help them defend their territories. Male pinks and sockeyes develop a pronounced hump on the back, just ahead of the dorsal fin. Their grotesque appearance may also intimidate predators and competing males that approach the spawning site.

Both sexes undergo dramatic color changes. Color shifts are different for the different species, but in most cases the colors become considerably darker and more intense. The most pronounced are in Pacific salmon. As spawning time approaches and their bodies begin to deteriorate, they change from bright silver to brilliant red, olive green, or even black.

SPAWNING SITE. Trout and salmon prefer a clean gravel bottom for spawning, usually at the tail of a pool or in some other area where the current sweeps the bottom free of silt.

The female digs the redd. She turns on her side and beats her tail against the bottom, moving the gravel away and creating a depression longer than her body and about half as deep.

As the female digs, she is often accompanied by more than one male; the largest male is dominant and defends his territory by charging the smaller ones, using his kype to nip them. A female commonly digs several redds, depositing a portion of her eggs in each.

SPAWNING ACT. The dominant male courts the female by nudging and quivering. Finally, the two lay side by side in the redd. They become rigid, arch their backs, and with their mouths agape, vibrate to release sperm and eggs. Sometimes, the other males also deposit sperm in the redd.

After spawning, the female digs at the upstream edge of the redd, covering the eggs with several inches of gravel. When all spawning activity is completed, the parents abandon the redd. Female Pacific salmon try to guard their redds for a short time, but they soon weaken and die. Salmonids do not attempt to guard their young after they hatch.

Male brook trout undergo a dramatic color change during spawning, changing from their normal coloration (top) to vividly pronounced colors (bottom).

Male Pacific salmon undergo astounding physical changes just prior to spawning.

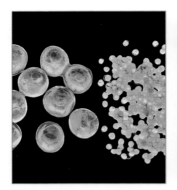

Salmon and trout produce fewer and larger eggs than most other freshwater gamefish. Salmon eggs (left) are much larger than walleye eggs (right).

All species of trout and salmon, except the golden trout, lose their parr marks as they mature.

EGGS AND INCUBATION. Trout and salmon are less prolific than most other gamefish. They have very large eggs, few in number. A 10-pound (4.5 kg) rainbow deposits only about 4,000 eggs; a walleye of the same size, for comparison, deposits about 200,000.

Salmonid eggs incubate from one to five months, depending on species. This long incubation period subjects the eggs to many hazards, such as disease and flooding. Predators such as crayfish, insects, and other fish, including trout, quickly eat eggs that are not well buried.

JUVENILE STAGES. The eggs hatch in the gravel, and at first the fry can move very little. They do not feed, but get nutrients from the attached yolk sac. After several weeks, they gain enough strength to wiggle through the gravel and emerge into the stream. Soon afterward, the fry absorb the yolk sac and begin feeding on plankton.

As the fish grow, they develop a row of dark, oval-shaped marks along the side. At this stage the fish are called parr; the markings are called parr marks.

In the case of anadromous fish like salmon and steelhead, the young spend at least six months, and sometimes as long as three years, in the home stream before they start to develop migratory tendencies. As the migratory urge develops, the parr marks start to disappear, the sides turn a brilliant silver, and the fish begin moving downstream. This process is called smolting, and the young at this stage are called smolts. The smolts spend several years at sea or in a large lake before reaching maturity.

Predation is severe during a trout's early life. Kingfishers, herons, otters, and fish take the greatest toll. As a rule, less than one percent of newly hatched fry survive to age one.

HOMING. Salmon are known for their uncanny ability to return to their home stream to spawn, swimming thousands of miles (km) across oceans and up rivers. Trout have the same ability to a lesser extent.

Although migratory salmonids sometimes stray to other rivers, the vast majority return to the same river, and usually to the precise area of that river, where they hatched years earlier.

Where spawning streams have been polluted or blocked by dams, salmon populations decline or disappear because the fish do not seek out alternative streams.

WHEN SALMONIDS SPAWN	
Species	**Time of Year**
Rainbow trout	Spring
Brown trout	Fall
Cutthroat trout	Spring
Golden trout	Midsummer
Brook trout	Early fall
Bull trout	Early fall
Dolly Varden	Fall
Arctic char	Fall
Arctic grayling	Early spring
Pink salmon	Fall
Chinook salmon	Fall
Coho salmon	Late fall
Chum salmon	Fall
Sockeye salmon	Fall
Atlantic salmon	Fall

HATCHERY TROUT VS. WILD TROUT

Hatchery trout (bottom) are easily distinguished from wild trout (top). They lack the brilliant coloration of wild trout, and in many cases their fins are worn from constant rubbing against the hatchery's concrete raceways.

To many trout enthusiasts, "hatchery trout" are dirty words. Whirling disease and other fish-killing viruses were originally linked to hatchery-reared fish. However, trout fishermen also realize that without hatchery-reared trout they would have fewer trout fishing opportunities.

There is no denying that hatchery-reared trout lack many of the desirable attributes of wild ones. They are much less wary and considerably easier for anglers and predators to catch. When hooked, they wage a comparatively weak battle and are much less likely to jump.

The main gripe against hatchery trout is that they compete for food and space with wild trout. Often, the size and number of trout in a stream increases dramatically when stocking is discontinued. Another problem is genetic contamination. When hatchery trout breed with wild ones, the offspring are less suited to the environment than the wild trout were.

Of course, hatcheries must stock streams that do not have suitable conditions for natural reproduction, if there is to be a trout fishery. Managers continue to stock catchable-size trout in many such put-and-take streams, particularly near large cities. Even so, the put-and-take management is gradually giving way to a put-and-grow philosophy; the trout are stocked as fry or fingerlings, and then allowed to grow up in the stream. This type of stocking is considerably less expensive, and the trout that survive to catchable size bear a much closer resemblance to wild trout.

HABITAT

Mention the term "trout stream," and most people think of flowing water that is cold, clear, and unpolluted. This stereotype is accurate, but there are other requirements as well. The quantity and size of trout a stream produces depend on the following:

WATER FERTILITY. A stream's fertility, or level of dissolved minerals, affects the production of plankton, the fundamental link in the aquatic food chain. The level of dissolved minerals depends mainly on the water source. Limestone streams generally have a considerably higher mineral content than freestone streams.

A limestone stream is normally fed by an underground spring rich in calcium carbonate, an important nutrient, and flows over a streambed that supplies even more minerals. Limestone streams have more aquatic vegetation, produce more insects and crustaceans, and generally grow more and larger trout.

A freestone stream is fed by runoff or springs with a low mineral content. It typically flows over a streambed that contributes few nutrients to the water. But some freestone streams pick up extra nutrients from fertile tributaries, so they produce good-sized trout.

WATER TEMPERATURE. All streams that support permanent trout populations have one thing in common: a reliable source of cold water.

The cold water often comes from springs or meltwater from snow or glaciers. Streams fed by ordinary surface runoff become too warm for trout in midsummer, except in the North or at high altitudes, where air temperatures stay cool all year.

Some trout can survive at surprisingly warm water temperatures. Browns and rainbows, for instance, live in streams where temperatures sometimes rise into the low 80s (27 to 29°C). Though at these temperatures they usually feed very little, their growth rate slows, and their resistance to disease diminishes.

The stream temperature depends not only on the water source, but also on the shape and gradient (slope) of the channel, and the amount of shade.

GRADIENT. The most productive trout streams have a relatively low gradient, from 0.5 to 2 percent, which converts to 25 to 100 feet (7.6 to 30.5 m) per mile (1.6 km). In other words, the streambed drops that

Silted or muddy streambeds produce few insects and are unsuitable for spawning.

Clean gravel or rubble streambeds are a good habitat for aquatic insects and provide the essential conditions required for spawning.

many feet for each mile of length. The higher the gradient, the faster the current flows.

Mountain streams may have a much higher gradient, sometimes as great as 15 percent. Above 7 percent, a stream must have stair-step pools, boulders, log jams, or other slack-water areas if it is to support trout.

A channel with a gradient less than 0.5 percent tends to have a silty bottom and water too warm for trout.

BOTTOM TYPE. A clean gravel or rubble bottom produces much more insect life than a sandy or silty bottom. It also makes a better spawning substrate.

Streambed siltation is a major problem facing many trout streams. Excess silt can result from logging, poor farming practices, and overgrazing of stream banks. The silt clogs up the spaces between the gravel, destroying insect habitat, and causing eggs deposited in the gravel to suffocate.

Conservation agencies often fence trout streams to keep out cattle, allowing vegetation to redevelop.

HABITAT DIVERSITY. A stream with diverse habitat generally produces more trout than one with uniform habitat throughout. Where the habitat is diverse, trout find a variety and abundance of food.

Many types of aquatic insects thrive in riffles and runs; baitfish and burrowing aquatic insects abound in pools. If a stream has aquatic vegetation like stonewort or watercress, the plants often host scuds, midge larvae, and other trout foods. Diverse habitat also provides plenty of resting and spawning areas.

Streams that meander in a snakelike pattern have greater habitat diversity than streams with a straight channel. Consequently, they have cover for trout that is more natural. As a stream winds along, banks along the outside bends become undercut and tree roots wash out, making ideal hiding spots.

Fisheries managers dread the prospect of stream channelization. They know that when the channel is artificially straightened, riffle-run-pool habitat disappears, and trout disappear with it.

SHAPE OF CHANNEL. A narrow, deep channel is generally better than a wide, shallow one. In the latter, a higher percentage of the water is exposed to the air and sun, causing the water to warm more rapidly.

Where the channel is too wide, there is not enough current to keep silt in suspension, so it settles out, smothering gravel beds that provide food and spawning habitat. Stream-improvement projects are often intended to narrow a channel that has been widened by eroding banks or beaver dams.

Meandering streams provide a diverse habitat for aquatic foods, critical cover, as well as resting and spawning areas.

Upper zone, or headwaters, normally has very cold water, a low flow, and a narrow streambed. The headwaters serve as a spawning and rearing area, but is too small to support large trout.

The middle zone has cool water and is the most productive part of the stream. It has the best insect populations and generally supports the highest population of adult trout.

The lower zone is generally warmer and the bottom may be silty or muddy. It supports the fewest trout, but may hold some of the largest ones, along with warmwater gamefish.

STABILITY OF FLOW. Almost any stream can support trout in spring, when water temperatures are cool and water flows are high. But trout must live in the stream year around. If the flow falls too low, even for a few days, trout will probably not survive.

Streams with a distinct cold water source commonly have temperature zones. The upper zone, or headwater, normally has very cold water, a low flow, and a narrow streambed. The headwater serves as a spawning and rearing area, but is too small to support large trout. Because of the cold water, it may hold brook trout. Along the stream course, tributaries flow in and increase the stream's size. The middle zone has cool water and is the most productive part of the stream. It has the best insect hatches and diversity, and generally supports the highest population of adult trout. As more tributaries flow in, the stream gets even larger and the streambed flattens out. The water is warm, the current is slow, and the bottom is silty. The lower zone supports few trout, but some of the largest ones. You may find big browns along with suckers, carp, and even catfish.

Low flows present the biggest problem in later summer, especially in areas with little forest cover to preserve ground moisture. If the weather is hot and there has been little rain, too much water evaporates from the stream, reducing the depth and slowing the current, so the remaining water warms faster. Even if trout survive the warm water, they are under so much stress that they do not feed. Low water can also be a problem in winter. In a dry year, winter flows may drop so low that the stream freezes to the bottom.

Large underground springs provide the most stability. They ensure at least a minimal flow so the stream doesn't dry up during a drought. And because spring water comes out of the ground at the same temperature year around, these streams stay cool in summer and relatively warm in winter.

SHADE. Most streams require some shade from trees or overhanging grasses to keep the water cool enough for trout. A stream that lacks sufficient shade will be cool enough in the upper reaches, but the water will warm rapidly as it moves downstream, so the trout zone is limited. A stream with too much shade may hold trout over most of its length, but the cold temperature inhibits food production and slows trout growth. Fisheries managers have found that they can maximize trout production by planting or removing trees to regulate the amount of shade.

WATER CLARITY. Most trout species prefer clear water, although some, like browns and rainbows, can tolerate low clarity. Clear water allows sunlight to penetrate to the streambed, promoting the growth of plants, which in turn produce trout food. Clear water also makes it easy for trout to see food and avoid predators, including anglers.

DISSOLVED OXYGEN. A lack of adequate dissolved oxygen is rarely a problem in trout streams, except in tailwater fisheries where cold, dense water from the depths of a reservoir must be aerated as it passes through the dam. In most streams, however, oxygen is replenished through contact with the air.

pH LEVEL. In most streams the exact pH level is of little importance to fishermen. Trout, like most fish, can tolerate a wide range of pH levels, and can live in waters with a pH as low as 4.5 or as high as 9.5. Nevertheless, extremely low pH levels resulting from acid rain have wiped out brook trout populations in parts of the Northeast. Many kinds of trout foods, like mayflies, are less tolerant of low pH levels than the trout themselves.

HABITAT PREFERENCES OF SALMONIDS	
Species	**Preferred Water Temp**
Rainbow trout	55-60°F (12.8–15.6°C)
Brown trout	60-65°F (15.6–18.3°C)
Cutthroat trout	55-62°F (12.8–16.7°C)
Golden trout	58-62°F (14.4–16.7°C)
Brook trout	52-56°F (11.1–13.3°C)
Bull trout	45-55°F (7.2–12.8°C)
Dolly Varden	50-55°F (10–12.8°C)
Arctic char	45-50°F (7.2–10°C)
Arctic grayling	42-50°F (5.6–10°C)
Pink salmon	52-57°F (11.1–13.9°C)
Chinook salmon	53-57°F (11.7–13.9°C)
Coho salmon	53-57°F (11.7–13.9°C)
Chum salmon	54-57°F (12.2–13.9°C)
Sockeye salmon	50-55°F (10–12.8°C)
Atlantic salmon	53-59°F (11.7–15°C)

Spring-fed tributaries cool the water below the point where they enter the stream. They attract trout in mid to late summer.

Undercut banks usually form along outside bends. They offer excellent midday cover, especially in sunny weather.

Riffles are morning and evening feeding areas. Trout and salmon usually spawn just above or below riffles, but may spawn right in them.

Runs, the deep, moderately fast moving areas between riffles and pools, hold trout almost anytime, if there is sufficient cover.

Pools are smoother and look darker than other areas of the stream. They make good midday resting spots for medium to large trout.

Brush piles offer good cover, break the current, and produce invertebrates for food. They usually hold small to medium trout.

Plunge pools are deep holes scoured out by falling water. They offer increased dissolved oxygen levels, and can be prime locations for good-sized trout.

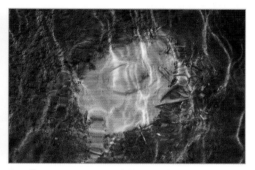

Upwelling springs appear as light spots of bubbling sand where the silt has been washed away. They draw trout in mid- to late summer.

Flats, slow-moving shallow areas, are morning and evening feeding areas. They normally lack the cover necessary to hold trout in midday.

Pocket water is shallow and has scattered boulders. It may appear too shallow, but the deep pockets below the boulders usually hold trout.

Typical Trout and Salmon Streams

Trout and salmon live in streams ranging in size from meadow brooks narrow enough to hop across, to major rivers large enough to carry oceangoing vessels. Described below are the most common types of trout and salmon streams, representing both the limestone and freestone categories:

FREESTONE STREAMS

Medium-gradient freestone streams, the most common trout stream type, have moderate current with numerous pools, riffles, and runs. The streambed is comprised mostly of large gravel, rubble, and boulders, and has some pocket water. Most medium-gradient freestone streams are fed by surface runoff and meltwater. Because the water carries few nutrients, these streams are relatively unproductive. However, many have large tributary systems that add enough nutrients to produce abundant food and large trout. The best of these streams have good spring flow, keeping water temperatures in the ideal range for trout feeding and growth.

High-gradient freestone streams, fed by snowmelt and surface runoff, are usually found in mountainous areas. The current is fast, with long stretches of pocket water but few pools. Because of the short food supply, trout usually run small but are willing biters.

Low-gradient freestone streams wind through bogs, meadows, or woodlands. They have sand or silt bottoms, and undercut banks or deadfalls for cover. Some, fed by springs or meltwater, have clear water; others, fed by swamp drainage, have tea-colored water.

LIMESTONE STREAMS

Low-gradient limestone streams have some spring flow, move slowly, and have a meandering streambed composed of silt, sand, or small gravel. The depth is fairly uniform, with few riffles. In meadow streams, a common variety, overhanging grass is the primary cover for trout.

Medium-gradient limestone streams normally have some spring flow, moderate to fast current, a pool-riffle-run configuration, and a streambed composed of gravel, rubble, or boulders. Many such streams flow over exposed limestone bedrock and have large numbers of crayfish.

OTHER COMMON STREAM TYPES

Tailwater streams, fed by cold water from the depths of a reservoir, produce trophy trout. The stream level may fluctuate greatly during the day as water is released to drive power turbines. This limits insect populations, but baitfish and crustaceans are plentiful.

Spring creeks, either limestone or freestone, arise from groundwater sources. They have slow to moderate current, very clear water, lush weed growth, and heavy insect populations. Some produce tremendous numbers of crustaceans and surprisingly large trout.

UNDERSTANDING MOVING WATER

Fast water in a riffle excavates a deeper channel, or run, immediately downstream. As current digs the run deeper, the velocity slows, forming a pool. Because of the slower current, sediment is deposited at the pool's downstream end, raising the streambed and channeling the water into a smaller area. Because the flow is more constricted, the current speeds up, forming another riffle. The sequence then repeats.

Why does a trout lie upstream of a boulder when there is a noticeable eddy on the downstream side? Why does it choose a feeding station on the bottom when most of its food is drifting on the surface? And why does a fly cast near the bank drift more slowly than a fly line in midstream?

Questions like these have a direct bearing on your ability to find and catch trout. Answering them correctly requires a basic understanding of stream hydraulics. The trout lies on the upstream side of the boulder because an eddy forms upstream of an object, as well as downstream.

The trout chooses a feeding station on the bottom because friction with bottom materials slows the current to as little as one-fourth the speed of the surface current. Similarly, the fly next to the bank drifts more slowly than the fly line in midstream because friction with the bank slows the current.

Understanding how moving water shapes the stream channel, and learning to recognize the resulting habitat types can also improve your chances of finding trout. In most good trout streams, the current creates a riffle-run-pool sequence that repeats itself along the stream course.

A deep pool may hold big brown trout, but rainbows and smaller browns are more likely to be found in runs. Riffles hold only small

Current speed varies within the stream cross-section. The blue area has slow current; the purple, moderate current; the red, fast current. Water in the fast zone moves up to four times as fast as water in the slow zone.

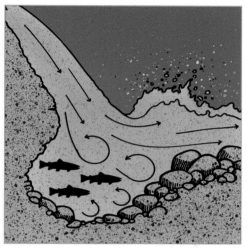

Eddies form both upstream and downstream of an obstacle such as a boulder. Many anglers do not realize that there is an eddy on the upstream side; they work only the downstream eddy, bypassing a lot of trout.

Plunge pools form at the base of a falls as a result of the cascading water. Plunge-pool depth usually exceeds the distance from the crest of the falls to the water level. A dugout often forms at the base of the falls.

trout during midday, but are important morning and evening feeding areas for most species. A normal stream tends to meander, or weave, as it flows downstream. Current flowing to the outside of a bend becomes swifter, eroding the streambed and sometimes carving an undercut bank. At the same time, current on the opposite side of the stream slackens, causing silt to settle out and fill in the streambed. In almost all cases, the outside bends hold the most trout.

Most stream fishermen know that water plunging over a falls digs out a pool at the base. But many do not realize that the turbulence caused by the plunging water undercuts the base of the falls, forming a cave that makes one of the best feeding and resting stations in the stream.

PARTS OF A STREAM

RIFFLE: Shallow water; fast current; turbulent surface; gravel, rubble, or boulder bottom. In big rivers, these areas are called rapids.

RUN: Deeper than a riffle, with moderate to fast current; surface not as turbulent; bottom materials range from small gravel to rubble.

POOL: Deep, slow-moving water with a flat surface; bottom of silt, sand, or small gravel. Similar but shallower areas are called flats.

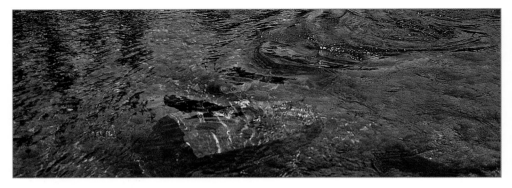

Boils form when the current deflects upward off an underwater obstruction, usually a boulder. When you see a boil, there is a good chance that trout are holding in the eddy just downstream of the obstruction. But the boil forms farther downstream, so you must cast well upstream of the boil to catch the trout.

Reading Water

An experienced stream angler can learn a great deal about a stream simply by walking its banks and "reading" the water. Current patterns, surface disturbances, coloration differences, changes in bottom type, and other clues reveal trout and salmon hiding spots.

Current patterns pinpoint the location of rocks, logs, or other underwater objects that shelter fish from the moving water. Current pushing against a bank may indicate an undercut that offers cover. The seam between fast and slow current makes a good feeding station; trout hold in the slower water waiting for food to drift by in the faster water.

Novice stream anglers often pass up any water where the surface is broken and ripply, mistakenly assuming it is too fast and too shallow for trout. However, if you look carefully, you may see that this water has slack-water pockets. A small pocket behind a rock might be home to a good-sized trout, even though the water is less than a foot (30 cm) deep.

Bottom makeup also dictates where trout will be found. A section of stream with a sandy bottom generally supports fewer trout than a section with a rocky or gravelly bottom. Important trout foods, especially larval aquatic insects, thrive among rocks and gravel, but may be completely absent in sand.

If possible, examine the stream from a high angle to get an idea of streambed contour and location of boulders, submerged logs, weed patches, and other underwater objects. You can see best on a bright day when the sun is at its highest. Polarized sunglasses will remove the glare so you can see into the water.

Many trout streams have been damaged by erosion, beaver activity, channelization, or logging. Natural resources agencies and outdoor clubs sometimes reclaim these streams by installing devices to deepen the channel and provide good cover for trout.

TIPS FOR READING WATER

Undercut banks can be found by watching the current. If it is angling toward a bank, rather than flowing parallel to it, the bank is undercut.

Deep holes appear as dark areas in the streambed. Trout move into holes to escape the current. The best holes have boulders or logs for cover.

Weed patches may be difficult to see, especially in low light. But the weeds usually slow the current, creating slack spots on the surface.

Current seams are easy to spot because debris and foam usually collect in the slack water, near the edge of the fast water.

Check your favorite stream at low-water stage to find deep holes and objects like submerged logs that could hold trout when the water is higher.

COMMON STREAM-IMPROVEMENT DEVICES

Crib shelters, man-made undercut banks supported by pilings, are built along outside bends. Water is deflected toward them by a rock or log structure on the opposite bank, scouring the bank under the crib. The left photo shows the shelter under construction, the right photo a year later.

Hewitt Ramps, used mainly on high-gradient streams, function much like small dams. A deeper pool forms above; a scour hole forms below.

WEATHER

Light rain or moderate wind disturbs the surface enough that trout cannot see you clearly. The fish feed heavily on terrestrial foods washed in by the rain or wind and are not nearly as spooky as they are when the surface is calm. But heavy rain pelting the surface or intense wind puts the trout down.

In stream fishing for trout and salmon, nothing is more important than weather. It affects the clarity, temperature, and water level of the stream, which largely determine where the fish will be found and how well they will bite.

The most important factor is rain. Trout often start to feed when the sky darkens before a storm. A light to moderate rain slightly clouds the water, washes terrestrial foods into the stream, increases the flow, and causes greater numbers of immature aquatic insects to drift downstream. These changes make ideal feeding conditions and good fishing. A heavy rain, on the other hand, seems to turn the fish off. If the downpour is prolonged, it muddies the water so much that the fish cannot see, and with the rising water, they abandon their normal locations.

Rain has even more effect on anadromous trout and salmon. Fish entering a stream to spawn tend to stage up at the stream mouth. A few will enter a stream at the normal flow, but the majority wait for the increased flow resulting from a heavy rain. Fishing is poor as long as the stream stays muddy, but improves rapidly when the water starts to clear.

Air temperature also has a dramatic effect on feeding activity. Most trout and salmon species feed heaviest at water temperatures from 55 to 60°F (12.8 to 15.6°C). On a typical stream, warm, sunny weather early or late in the season will drive the water temperature to that range by midafternoon, triggering an insect hatch and starting a feeding spree. But in summer the same type of weather warms the water too much by midafternoon, so fishing is poor. Then, trout bite better in the morning or evening, when the water is cooler.

Another important element is cloud cover. In sunny weather, trout are extra wary, seeking the cover of boulders, logs, or undercut banks. In cloudy weather, they are more aggressive and more willing to leave cover to find food. Anadromous fish tend to migrate more under cloudy skies.

Windy weather also makes trout more aggressive. The wind blows insects into the stream and the trout start feeding. However, trout have difficulty spotting small insects when the surface is choppy, so dry-fly fishing is not as effective as it would be if the water were calm.

GOOD CONDITIONS FOR TROUT FISHING

Overcast skies eliminate harsh shadows that can spook trout. The fish do not hesitate to leave cover to search for food, sometimes moving into riffles in midday.

Slightly murky water allows trout to see the lure, but makes it difficult for them to see you. The clarity is best when the stream is rising or after it starts to fall.

Chapter 2
EQUIPMENT

Whether you're fishing with fly or spinning gear, having the right equipment can make the difference between a successful fishing trip and a disappointing one. Choosing the right gear doesn't have to be difficult, and shouldn't keep you from pursuing trout and salmon.

In this section you'll learn how to choose the proper fly line, select the right fly rod and reel, and select the right leader. You'll also learn how to choose the right spinning or baitcasting rod, reel, and line.

After all of your preparation for a day's fishing trip, the last thing you want is to reel in a broken line and not be prepared to fix it on site. The charts in this section give you helpful line weight stats at a glance. And then photos show you uses for specific scenarios. With this information you'll be able to better plan and you'll be better prepared to handle some of the inevitable situations that can occur on fishing day.

Next, we'll show you how to identify and select the appropriate accessories and tools to help you perform the little tasks such as adding tippet, weighting nymphs, keeping dry flies afloat, and checking water temperature.

Choosing the right fishing gear shouldn't be intimidating. In fact, it's the first step toward actually getting out on the water.

FLY RODS & REELS

Rods

In spinning and baitcasting, it's important to select the right rod, but the selection is not as critical as in fly fishing. A fly rod propels the line, which in turn propels the fly; if the rod is not matched to the line, casting is next to impossible. When choosing a fly rod, consider the following:

MATERIAL. In the late 1940s, fiberglass rods revolutionized fly fishing. They were considerably less expensive than the old bamboo rods, yet lighter and stiffer, so they could handle a fly line more easily. With the introduction of graphite in 1972, rod-building technology took another quantum leap.

Today's graphite rods weigh 20 to 25 percent less than glass rods of the same stiffness, and 40 to 45 percent less than bamboo. Consequently, graphite rods can be longer and lighter, yet more powerful. And you can cast farther with less effort.

Because of the obvious advantages of graphite, fewer and fewer glass rods are produced these days. For those who enjoy the romance of fishing with a bamboo rod, there are many manufacturers and custom rod makers still building them. Some old bamboo rods have become collector items, commanding prices well into the thousands of dollars. Bamboo has enjoyed resurgence in popularity over the last decade or two, and it's doubtful bamboo rods ever will go out of style.

POWER. For peak casting performance, the power or stiffness of your fly rod should match the weight of your fly line. If the rod is too light, it will flex too much and lose its casting power. Too heavy, and it will not flex enough to propel the line.

Most fly rods have a line weight printed near the grip. As a rule, you can use line one size lighter or heavier than the recommended weight.

ROD ACTION. The word "action" may be the most misused term among anglers. Some confuse action with power; others say "this rod has a nice action," meaning that it feels good in the hand.

In reality, two different characteristics determine "action." The first is where the rod bends under a load. The second is how quickly it recovers from a bend, or dampens. These characteristics are determined by the design of the taper of the rod, and the material with which the rod is made. Slow-action rods bend almost throughout their entire length, and recover slowly from a bend. Fast-action rods flex most near the tip, and recover quickly from a bend. In most cases, the fastest-action bamboo rod will feel considerably slower than even a slow-action graphite rod.

A faster rod forms a narrower loop, which travels more rapidly and has less air resistance, resulting in greater distance and accuracy. Faster rods also "dampen" more quickly after the cast, so the tip doesn't bounce and throw waves into the line. Waves in the line increase air resistance, reduce distance, and cause a sloppy delivery.

A slower rod absorbs more shock, a big advantage when fishing dry flies with light tippets. A slower rod makes it easier to control casting distance. Because the loop is not as narrow, the line speed is slower, so you can easily stop the line when the fly is over the target. Nonetheless, the wide loop reduces casting distance considerably.

Unfortunately, there are no industry standards to designate action, and some rod makers don't even try. One manufacturer's "slow" rod may have the same action as another's "medium" rod. An experienced tackle-shop employee can help you make your decision.

LENGTH. A 7½- to 9-foot (2.3 to 2.7 m) fly rod suits most trout fishing situations, but longer and shorter rods also have their uses.

In the past, anglers shied away from longer rods because they were too heavy. Today's graphite rods are so light that greater lengths are becoming popular. Long rods give you more casting power, make it easier to mend the line, and help you keep your back cast high enough to avoid streamside brush. Also, with the rod tip high it's easier to control your line and fly on the drift. Salmon anglers often use two-handed rods called Spey rods, named for Scotland's legendary Spey River, up to 15 feet (4.6 m) in length, for making long casts, controlling the line on the water, and handling these powerful fish.

Short rods are easier to handle on narrow, brushy streams. They also make it easier to place a fly beneath an overhang, and to land trout in tight spots. Anglers on brush-lined creeks sometimes use fly rods as short as 6 feet (1.8 m).

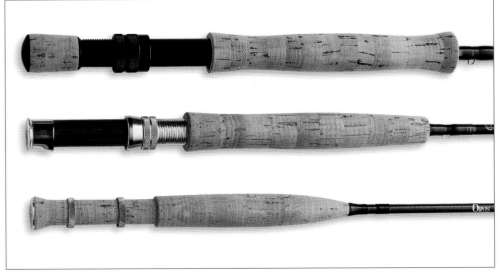

Reel seats include (top) down-locking, used on light rods; (middle) up-locking, used on heavier rods to prevent unscrewing, and for more length behind the reel so the spool won't rub clothing; (bottom) sliding-band, to reduce weight on bamboo rods and light graphite rods.

Grips include (bottom) cigar, for short- to medium-range casting with light rods; (middle) half Wells, with a thicker front for more casting leverage and a raised middle for a better grip; (top) full Wells, with a raised front for even more casting leverage, and a raised middle.

Reels

Choosing a fly reel is not nearly as complicated as choosing the right fly rod or line. The reel serves primarily to store the line, and to provide drag tension when a fish makes a long run. When selecting a fly reel, consider the following:

REEL ACTION. The action of a reel is the way it retrieves line. With a single-action reel, the spool turns once for each turn of the handle; with a multiplying reel, it turns more than once.

Single-action reels are adequate for most trout fishing. Multiplying reels, though heavier, are better for powerful fish like steelhead. They allow you to take up slack in a hurry should a fish run toward you. Both actions are highly reliable.

Most fly reels will accommodate a range of line weights.

Both types of reels are also available in direct-drive and anti-reverse models. Direct drives are more common; the handle turns when the spool does, so if a big fish takes line, the handle turns backward. Should you accidentally touch the whirling handle, your tippet would snap. On anti-reverse models, the handle does not turn backward with the spool.

DRAG. When a big trout grabs your fly and rockets away, you'll need a good drag to prevent spool overrun, and to tire the fish. The simplest type of drag is the ratchet-and-pawl. An adjustable spring keeps the pawl pressed against the ratchet and makes an audible click. Disc-style drags perform like the brakes on a car, using smooth friction of one large surface against another. Both are adjusted with a knob on the side of the reel. Many reels have an exposed spool rim, which allows you to apply additional drag tension by pressing your palm against the rim, called palming.

CAPACITY AND WEIGHT. The reel you choose should be designed to hold the size fly line you've selected with ample capacity for backing material. The larger the fish you're after, the greater the capacity you'll need. Check the capacity information listed in the literature that comes with the reel to be sure it can hold the required line and backing.

ARBOR. The arbor is the center axis of the reel spool, to which you tie the backing. Once the backing has filled the reel to the proper capacity, the fly line is tied to the backing, and the balance of the reel is filled. Fly reels traditionally have had a narrow center axis, or arbor. Reel designers discovered that by increasing the diameter and width of the reel's arbor, the reel takes up line more quickly. These reels, called "large-arbor," are popular with anglers pursuing large trout and salmon. Mid-arbor reels combine the added backing capacity of traditional narrow-arbor reels with the faster take-up of large arbor reels, and are most common on big-game reels.

FLY LINE

The fly line distinguishes fly fishing from all other forms of fishing, and makes it possible to cast an essentially weightless fly. The weight of the line bends, or loads, the rod, propelling the line, leader, and fly.

A well-stocked tackle shop offers a wide assortment of fly lines. They come in different weights, different tapers, and a selection of colors. Some float, some sink, and some do a little of each. Choosing the right lines for various situations need not be difficult. Your decision depends mainly on the weight designation of your fly rod, and the size of your fly. It also depends on how far you want to cast, and how deep you want to fish. Other factors that may influence your selection include the trout's wariness, the water's surface (smooth or broken), and the amount of wind.

Most fly lines are 80 to 100 feet (24.4 to 30.5 m) long, consisting of a core of braided nylon or Dacron with a plastic coating. The plastic may be impregnated with tiny air bubbles or metal powder to make it float or sink, and it may vary in thickness so that the line tapers. When selecting and using fly lines, consider the following:

LINE WEIGHT. Every fly line is designed to conform to precise weight standards set by the tackle industry. This means that every 5-weight line—whether it sinks or floats—weighs exactly the same over the first 30 feet (9.1 m) of the line. This precise weight designation assures rod manufacturers that each of their rods can be designed to cast a specific weight line. Line weight is measured in grains, an ancient British measurement based on the weight of a grain of barley.

Practically all trout and salmon fishing is done with line weights 2 to 12.

Light-weight lines (2 to 4) give you the most delicate presentation. With line this light you can cast small, unweighted flies, but you cannot cast as far, and casting in a strong wind may be difficult.

Medium-weight lines (5 to 7) are the most versatile. They can handle flies of almost any size, and perform well in most fishing situations.

Heavy-weight lines (8 and 9) can deliver large flies and punch through the wind. Shooting-head lines are most often used in weights of 8 or heavier.

Extra-heavy lines (10 to 15) are used mainly for steelhead and salmon. Most lead-core shooting heads do not carry standard weight designations, but usually are cast with 10-weight rods. In Europe, anglers use 11- and 12-weight lines with two-handed salmon rods, but these are less popular in North America.

LINE TAPER. A fly line that tapers, or varies in diameter along its length, casts more efficiently than a level line. The forward section, or front taper, is thin at the tip but expands to a thicker section called the belly. The length and position of the belly determine how far and how delicately a given line will cast.

FLY LINE NUMBER DESIGNATION AND WEIGHT IN GRAINS

Number Designation	Standard Weight in grains (grams)	
1-Weight	60	(3.89 g)
2-Weight	80	(5.18 g)
3-Weight	100	(6.48 g)
4-Weight	120	(7.78 g)
5-Weight	140	(9.07 g)
6-Weight	160	(10.36 g)
7-Weight	185	(11.98 g)
8-Weight	210	(13.61 g)
9-Weight	240	(15.55 g)
10-Weight	280	(18.14 g)
11-Weight	330	(21.38 g)
12-Weight	380	(24.62 g)
13-Weight	450	(29.16 g)
14-Weight	500	(32.40 g)
15-Weight	550	(35.64 g)

With weight-forward (WF) line, the belly is short and near the forward end, so it shoots out easily, pulling the thinner running line with it. Weight-forward lines are the best choice for beginners. They are good for distance casting, but do not roll cast well.

On double-taper (DT) line, the belly is long and in the middle of the line; both ends taper equally. A double-taper line does not cast as far as a weight-forward, but is easier to mend and more economical; you can reverse it when one end wears out.

The shooting head or shooting taper (ST) is a special-purpose line that consists of about 30 feet (9.1 m) of level or tapered fly line, loop-spliced to 100 feet (30.5 m) of 15- to 30-pound (6.8 to 13.6 kg) mono running line. The mono is usually flattened or oval-shaped to minimize coiling. The heavy head easily pulls the mono, so you can cast extreme distances. They lack delicacy, and the long running line tangles easily. To minimize tangling, use a shooting basket or substitute a special thin fly line for the mono. Using the thin fly line reduces casting distance.

BUOYANCY. Floating lines (designated by the letter F) are the obvious choice for fishing dry flies. Because the line floats high on the surface film, little effort is required to pick it up for another cast, or to mend it. Floating lines can also be used with sinking flies, with or without added weight such as split shot or lead leader-wrap. With a floating line and a long leader, you can fish a sinking fly several feet (m) down.

Sinking lines (S) come in different densities, ranging from slow sinking to extremely fast sinking, for different depths, current speeds, and retrieve speeds. Because they sink over their entire length, they are difficult to control in current, and you must retrieve most of the line in order to make another cast. As a rule, use a sinking line whenever you are fishing deeper than 10 feet (3 m).

Sink tip lines, also called floating/sinking lines (F/S), have 5 to 20 feet (1.5 to 6.1 m) of sinking line attached to a floating line. Generally, the sinking portion is a different color. The sink rate of the tip ranges from

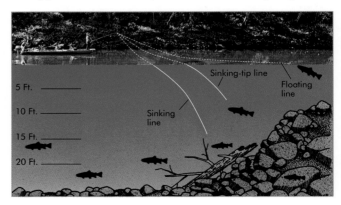

5 Ft. — _____

10 Ft. _____

15 Ft. _____

20 Ft. _____

Sinking-tip line

Floating line

Sinking line

intermediate to extremely fast. Because only the tip sinks, these lines are easier than sinking lines to pick up from the water. They work well at depths of 2 to 10 feet (0.61 to 3 m).

LINE DESIGNATIONS. When you purchase a fly line, look for a three-part code on the label that designates the taper, weight, and flotation of the line. The code WF-06-F, for instance, designates a weight-forward, 6-weight, floating fly line.

MATCHING ROD TO LINE. The weight of your line determines the power of the rod needed to handle it. If you try to cast a light line with a heavy rod, the rod will not flex enough to load. If you try to cast a heavy line with a light rod, the rod will flex too much to propel it. Most rods, however, will handle a line one weight either side of the recommended weight.

Backing helps prevent a fish from running out all your fly line.

Unfortunately, there is no standard way to measure rod power, so considerable variation exists among manufacturers. A 7-weight rod from one manufacturer may have the same power as a 5-weight rod from another. A good fly-fishing shop can help you sort out these differences.

Another complication is that line weight is measured by the weight of only the front 30 feet (9.1 m); no consideration is given to the rest of the line. The middle portion of a double-taper line, for instance, is thicker and heavier than the same portion of a weight-forward line. So you should select a double-taper line one size lighter than a weight-forward line for the same rod.

LINE COLOR. The color of a fly line is a matter of personal preference. Some fly casters prefer floating lines in bright colors because they are easiest to see, while others choose lines in subtle grays and greens to avoid spooking trout in clear spring creeks. Sinking lines, however, usually come in various shades of brown, green, or gray. In most types of fly fishing, the leader is long enough that the fish do not notice the color of the line.

BACKING. To keep a big fish from running out all your line, always use backing under your fly line. Backing also keeps your spool full so you can reel up line more quickly, and it minimizes coiling. Most trout fishermen use 20-pound (9 kg) braided Dacron.

Most reel manufacturers print the recommended amount of backing for each line weight right on the box, to take the guesswork out of spooling on the backing.

LINE CARE. If your line gets dirty or oily, simply wash it with mild soap. Floating lines need more care; use a commercial line cleaner to condition them. The line will stay pliable, float better, and shoot through the guides easier. Store your line where it will not be exposed to sunlight. Practice casting on grass or water; pavement will scuff your line. Gasoline and insect repellent can also damage the line's surface.

FLY LEADERS

The leader creates a nearly invisible connection between the heavy fly line and the fly. It also transfers the energy of the cast smoothly and efficiently, and helps give the fly a lifelike action on or in the water. The following components are important in leader selection.

MATERIAL. Until the 1950s, fly leaders were made from silkworm gut, which was strong and had low visibility, but became stiff and brittle when dry. Gut leaders required overnight soaking to make them supple enough for fishing.

Modern leaders come in a variety of man-made materials, which require far less care.

Nylon monofilament, the most popular leader material, is inexpensive, durable, and nearly invisible, with excellent knot strength. However, monofilament breaks down quickly in sunlight, and absorbs water, causing it to weaken.

Polyvinylidene fluoride (PVDF) material, commonly called "fluorocarbon," is even less visible in water than nylon, because its refractive properties, or the way light rays bend as they pass through it, more closely match the refractive properties of water. It has greater abrasion resistance but less stretch, requiring a more gentle hookset to prevent break offs with light tippets. Fluorocarbon is not affected by sunlight, and it will not absorb water. However, it costs more and has poorer knot strength than mono.

TAPER. Most leaders taper from a relatively thick butt section to a fine tippet. This taper ensures that the leader turns over easily and presents only the narrow-diameter tippet to the fish.

Fly leaders consist of a gradually tapering butt (about 60 percent of leader length), a rapidly tapering transition section (about 20 percent of length), and a level tip section or tippet (about 20 percent of length).

Modern tapered leaders come in two styles: knotted and knotless. A knotted leader normally has three to eight sections of monofilament of different diameters, tied together with blood knots. To ensure that the energy of the cast is transferred smoothly from line to leader, the thickest part of the leader butt should measure 0.017 inch (0.04 cm) for 2- to 4-weight fly line, 0.019 inch (0.048 cm) for 5- to 7-weight line, and 0.021 inch (0.053 cm) for line weights of 8 or over. For good knot strength, adjacent sections should differ in diameter by no more than 0.002 inch (0.0051 cm).

A knotted leader can be modified to suit your needs, and worn sections can be cut out and new ones tied in. However, the knots will weaken the leader and may pick up bits of weeds or debris.

Knotless leaders, by far the most popular, are stronger and do not catch debris. But if they do not have the right taper to turn over smoothly, there is little you can do but tie on a different leader.

With any leader, the tippet becomes shorter as new flies are tied on and worn sections are cut off. Rather than replacing the whole leader when the tippet becomes too short, simply replace the tippet. You can buy tippet material in 25-yard (22.9 m) spools.

HOW TO MAKE A KNOTTED LEADER

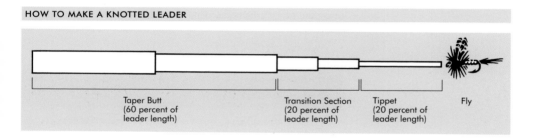

Taper Butt
(60 percent of
leader length)

Transition Section
(20 percent of
leader length)

Tippet
(20 percent of
leader length)

Fly

LENGTH. The length of your leader depends on the type of fly you plan to use. A sinking fly, when fished with a sinking or sink tip line, requires a short leader, from 3 to 4 feet (0.9 to 1.2 m). Strikes on sinking flies may be difficult to detect, and a short leader gives you a more direct connection. A short leader also pulls the fly deeper. A dry or sinking fly fished with a floating line requires a long leader, from 7½ to 12 feet (2.3 to 3.7 m).

With dry flies, the long leader can be manipulated to alight in a series of S-curves. This way, the fly floats freely for a longer time before drag sets in. A long tippet is especially important to ensure a drag-free drift.

TIPPET DIAMETER. A tippet's diameter is measured using a system developed in the days of silkworm gut leaders. The gut was drawn through a series of decreasing-size holes in metal plates, reducing its diameter. Each draw earned it another X (or mathematical times symbol; in other words, "4X" meant "drawn four times"). Even today, a tippet's X rating indicates diameter, not its breaking strength; the same X-rating may have different strengths depending on the manufacturer and material. The higher the X-rating number, the smaller the diameter.

The proper tippet diameter depends on the size of your fly. Always use the lightest tippet that will cast the fly efficiently.

Leader length and tippet diameter also depend on the size of the stream, the clarity of the water, and the wind conditions, as well as the size and wariness of the fish. On a very small stream or in windy weather, you may need a shorter-than-normal leader. On a very clear stream, or when trout are extra wary, your leader should be longer than normal. A heavy tippet improves your chances of landing a big trout, but reduces your odds of getting the fish to strike in the first place.

LEADER CARE. Mono leaders require little care, but you should store them in a lightproof package and check their strength and pliability before using. Heat, sunlight, or fluorescent light can weaken the leader and make it brittle. Check your leader often for nicks and abrasion. Replace your leader or tippet section if it develops a wind knot or abrasion. A small knot can reduce line strength by as much as 50 percent.

TIPPET SIZE CHART

Tippet Size	Diameter in Inches	Fly Size	Pound Test
0X	0.011 (0.0279 cm)	2-1/0	6.5–15.5 (2.95–7.05 kg)
1X	0.010 (0.0254 cm)	2-6	5.5–13.5 (2.5–6.14 kg)
2X	0.009 (0.0229 cm)	4-8	4.5–11.5 (2.05–5.23 kg)
3X	0.008 (0.0203 cm)	8-12	3.8–8.5 (1.73–3.86 kg)
4X	0.007 (0.0178 cm)	10-14	3.1–5.5 (1.41–2.5 kg)
5X	0.006 (0.0152 cm)	12-16	2.4–4.5 (1.09–2.05 kg)
6X	0.005 (0.0127 cm)	16-20	1.4–3.5 (0.63–1.59 kg)
7X	0.004 (0.0102 cm)	20-24	1.1–2.5 (0.5–1.14 kg)
8X	0.003 (0.0076 cm)	24-28	0.75–1.75 (0.34–.79 kg)

Tippets of the same diameter vary in strength depending on the brand of monofilament.

SPINNING & BAITCASTING TACKLE

Stream trout anglers use a variety of spinning and baitcasting tackle for fishing hardware and natural-bait rigs. Here are some guidelines for selecting rods, reels, and line:

Rods

All graphite rods are not the same. Some have considerably higher graphite content, and there are different types of graphite materials. You will get noticeably better performance from rods made of extra stiff, or high modulus, graphite. The rods most commonly used in stream trout fishing include:

LIGHT SPINNING. In small streams, anglers commonly use light to ultralight spinning rods with 2- to 6-pound (0.9 to 2.7 kg) mono. Most rods for this type of fishing measure $4\frac{1}{2}$ to $5\frac{1}{2}$ feet (1.37 to 1.67 m) in length, have a medium action, and are designed for lures from $\frac{1}{32}$ to $\frac{3}{8}$ ounce (0.89 g to 10.6 g). A medium-action rod flexes enough to cast most light lures and baits, yet has enough backbone for a good hookset. To cast extremely light lures, you need a slow-action rod.

MEDIUM SPINNING. These work best in medium to large streams with good-sized trout. They will easily handle $\frac{1}{4}$- to $\frac{5}{8}$-ounce (7.1 to 17.7 g) lures, which are needed for adequate casting distance and getting to the bottom. A typical outfit for this situation includes a 6- to 7-foot (1.8 to 2.1 m) medium-action rod and 6- to 8-pound (2.7 to 3.6 kg) mono.

Light spinning gear works well on small streams where brush or trees restrict your casting motion. A sidearm or backhand casting stroke places your lure beneath the branches.

Medium spinning gear is the best choice for wider, deeper, or faster-moving streams. Here, heavier lures are often necessary to make long casts and to reach bottom in the swift current.

Salmon and steelhead gear is needed to handle large salmonids in big rivers. The long, stiff rod gives you extra casting distance and more leverage for turning a powerful fish.

STEELHEAD AND SALMON. A long, stiff rod, combined with a high-capacity reel, is ideal for casting long distances. This type of rod also gives you more control of the line, better sensitivity, and more power for tiring the fish.

Some rod manufacturers now produce a line of steelhead and salmon rods that includes both spinning and baitcasting models. Most of these rods measure 8 to 10 feet (2.44 to 3.05 m) in length. They will handle lures from ½ to 2 ounces (14.2 to 56.7 g) and mono from 10- to 20-pound (4.5 to 9.1 kg) test. For drift fishing, steelhead and salmon fishermen often match an 8- to 9-foot (2.4 to 2.7 m) fly rod with a spinning reel.

Reels

Make sure your spinning reel has a large-diameter spool and a smooth drag. On many spinning reels, the spool is so small that even limp mono tends to coil. For a light or ultralight rod, spool diameter should be at least 1½ inches (3.8 cm); for a medium-power rod, 1¾ inches (4.5 cm); for a steelhead rod, 2 inches (5.1 cm).

A smooth drag is important in any stream fishing; if your drag sticks, even a small trout can snap your line in fast current. As a rule, front drags are smoother than rear drags. If possible, test the drag by attaching a 6- to 8-ounce (170 to 227 g) weight to the line, lifting the weight off the ground, then gradually loosening the drag. The weight should drop slowly and evenly; if it drops in jerks, look for another reel.

The drag is equally important on a baitcasting reel. Cheap reels often have "all-or-nothing" drags. When set light, the drag slips so much you can't set the hook. If you tighten it, it grabs too much and a big fish will break your line.

LINE. Trout are extremely line-shy, so most anglers use clear mono, or mono shaded to match the color of the water. Fluorescent line or other high-visibility line is not recommended. Hard-finish lines are popular for drift fishing because they can take more abrasion, but they're too stiff for most trout fishing. Limp mono works better for casting light lures and baits; it has less memory, meaning it is not as likely to form coils that reduce casting distance. But limp mono nicks easier, so you must retie hooks and lures more often.

TROUT FISHING ACCESSORIES

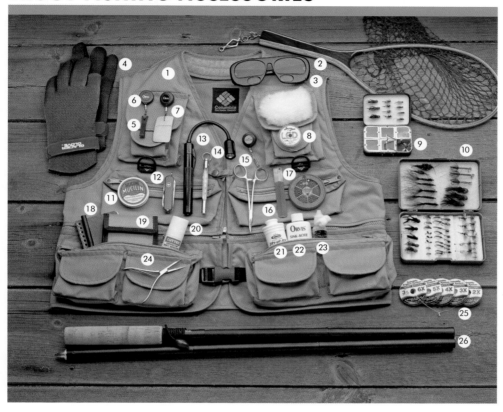

When you're wading a trout stream, you may walk a mile (1.6 km) or more from your starting point. Should you forget something, it's a long walk back to your car. Wear a fishing vest with lots of pockets and carry your accessories with you. You probably won't need all the accessories described below, but this list may give you some ideas.

CLIPPERS. Ordinary fingernail clippers work for cutting line, but specially designed clippers are better. They stay sharper longer, and have a small pin for cleaning head cement out of fly hook eyes.

CREEL. Canvas or wicker creels are best; when you wet them, evaporation keeps the fish cool.

FINGERLESS GLOVES. These gloves keep your hands warm and dry, yet allow you to tie knots. The warmest ones are made of neoprene.

FLY BOX. Dry flies should be stored in a box with large compartments to avoid crushing the delicate hackle. A box that has compartments

Trout fishing accessories include: (1) fishing vest, (2) landing net with French snap, (3) polarized sunglasses, (4) neoprene gloves, (5) line clipper on (6) retractor reel, (7) leader straightener on retractor, (8) leader wrap, (9) fly box with spring-loaded lids, (10) large, foam-lined fly box, (11) floatant, (12) Swiss Army knife, (13) gooseneck light, (14) water thermometer, (15) forceps on retractor, (16) hook file, (17) split shot assortment, (18) notebook and pen, (19) leader wallet, (20) insect repellent, (21) silicone fly desiccant, (22) leader sink, (23) fly line cleaner, (24) needle-nose pliers, (25) tippet material, (26) wading staff.

with individual spring-loaded lids protects your flies better from wind and rain. With other flies, the type of box is less critical. Some boxes have metal clips to hold the flies, but the clips are usually too large to hold flies smaller than size 14. Some boxes are magnetic, and in others the flies are embedded in foam; the foam boxes are best for tiny flies. Traditional fleece-lined fly books are still used, but if a fly is stored wet, the fleece absorbs moisture and the hook rusts.

FLOATANT. Silicone floatants in paste, liquid, or spray keep a dry fly floating longer.

FORCEPS. This tool is best for removing hooks from smaller trout.

HOOK HONE. Fly hooks are easily damaged by bumping rocks. The point can be resharpened with a small jewelry file or stone.

INSECT NET. A net is used to scoop insects from the water for identification. A small aquarium net will do. Some anglers carry small bottles so they can take the insects home for study.

INSECT REPELLENT. Stick repellent is best. Avoid lotion types that adhere to your hands; they could damage your fly line.

LANDING NET. Choose a net with a short handle and cotton mesh. Cotton is softer and less abrasive than synthetic material, so it's the best choice for catch-and-release fishing. Attach the net to your vest with a French clip, so you can detach it quickly.

LEADER SINK. Apply to a leader when using wet flies or nymphs.

LEADER STRAIGHTENER. The most popular type of straightener is a piece of leather, lined with silicone-treated rubber. Squeeze your tippet in the rubber and pull it through to remove any kinks or curls.

LEADER WALLET. Use wallets for storing extra leaders. Choose a wallet with zip-lock plastic holders.

LEADER WRAP. The flat lead wire can be wrapped on your leader as a substitute for split shot.

LINE CLEANER. Remove dirt and oil from your fly line.

NEEDLE-NOSE PLIERS. Use this tool for removing hooks from large trout and for flattening barbs in catch-and-release fishing. Select a small, lightweight model, preferably made of stainless steel.

NOTEBOOK. Use a notebook to record information on insect hatches and other streamside observations that could be useful in future years.

POLARIZED GLASSES. Polarized glasses reduce glare so you can see both bottom features and fish. Glass lenses resist scratching better than plastic. Prescription polarized lenses are available at most eyewear stores. You can also get glasses with small magnifying lenses for examining small objects.

PRIEST. Used for quickly killing trout you wish to keep.

RAIN JACKET. Keep a rain parka in the back of your vest.

RETRACTOR REEL. Reel with retractable cord for attaching clippers, forceps, or other accessories. The reel pins to your vest.

SILICONE POWDER. This drying agent quickly removes water or fish slime from a dry fly and reshapes the hackle. Place your fly in the container and shake; the powder will absorb the water.

SPLIT SHOT. A fly with split shot 6 to 12 inches (15.2 to 30.5 cm) ahead of it swims more naturally than one with lead wire on the hook shank. Also used for drifting live bait.

STOMACH PUMP. A pump is used for extracting stomach contents from trout you wish to release.

SWISS ARMY KNIFE. The knife blade can be used for gutting trout, the scissors for trimming hackle, the screwdriver for fixing a reel, the tweezers for examining insects, the toothpick for tying a nail knot.

TAPE MEASURE. For their personal records, many fishermen like to measure their trout before releasing them. Where length regulations apply, you may need to measure a trout to determine if it is legal size. A small tape measure will do, but you can also buy adhesive-backed tapes that stick to the butt section of your fly rod.

TIPPET MATERIAL. Carry tippet spools in all common diameters.

VEST. Your vest needs pockets to carry gear for a day's fishing, including raingear. Look for a vest with zippers on the large pockets, Velcro fasteners on the small ones, and a ring or loop at the rear of the collar for attaching a landing net. Make sure the vest is large enough that you can wear a heavy sweater underneath. Short vests are available for wading in deep water, and vests with mesh backs and shoulders are available for hot weather.

VEST LIGHT. A light helps when changing flies, unhooking fish, and finding your way in the dark. Select one with a clip that attaches to your vest, and with a gooseneck for directing the light.

WADING STAFF. A staff helps keep your balance in fast current. Collapsible staffs made of aluminum tubing are easy to carry in your vest, but wooden staffs are also popular.

WATER THERMOMETER. Select a fast-registering thermometer, preferably one with a metal tube. Use a cord long enough to reach the bottom.

Chapter 3

STREAM FISHING BASICS

Fishing in streams presents a new set of challenges. Trout are among the wariest of gamefish. Any quick movement or unusual sound, like the crunching of gravel or clattering of loose rocks when you wade, will send them darting for cover. And even when you do get them on line, you want to be prepared to walk the stream until they tire.

There are basic steps that will help you fish streams with success, and depending on the size and topography of the stream and its surrounding area different techniques will come in handy. In this chapter you will discover these techniques.

First you'll learn the basics of wading in streams. Various stream conditions require different techniques. Then you'll learn how to hook, play, and successfully land trout. These techniques will help you catch trout in any stream and in any weather.

Due to heavy fishing pressure on popular streams, conservation agencies now widely implement catch-and-release regulations. With such requirements enforced, it is important to address safe handling techniques to ensure future fishing. This is the final discussion in this chapter before moving on to fly fishing in Chapter 4.

WADING

In small, narrow streams, you will probably want to fish from the bank to conceal yourself, but you can fish most other streams more easily by wading. When you wade, your profile is lower, your back cast is less obstructed, and you can get closer to midstream lies. To wade effectively and safely, keep these suggestions in mind:

- Don't step off the bank without first checking the depth; if possible, cross at a riffle.

- Wear felt-soled waders or stream cleats for traction. Rubber soles are far too slippery for wading over wet, algae-covered rocks.

- Step softly to avoid banging rocks together. Before putting your full weight on a rock, make sure the rock is stable so it doesn't clink against other rocks or make you lose your balance.

- Walk with short, shuffling steps to keep ripples to a minimum on quiet pools, and to feel an uneven bottom better.

- In most situations, wade upstream. Trout face into the current, so you will be approaching them from behind and not stirring up silt that will drift over them. Also, it's safer to wade upstream; if you trip, the current helps hold you up. If you wade downstream, the current may push you too fast, causing you to lose your balance.

- To move from one spot to another along a stream, walk on the bank instead of wading in the streambed and disturbing the fish.

- Wear polarized glasses; they help you to spot fish and to avoid obstructions that could trip you.

TIPS FOR SAFE WADING

Carry a wading staff to help keep your balance in fast water or on a boulder-strewn bottom. A collapsible staff can be carried in your vest.

Turn sideways when wading in fast current. This minimizes the force of the current, so your feet are not swept out from under you.

Pivot upstream to turn around in fast current. If you pivot downstream, the current pushes you too fast, tending to wash you off your feet.

HOOKING, PLAYING & LANDING TROUT

The light lines and leaders used by most trout fishermen can easily result in a break-off, unless you know how to hook, play, and land the fish properly.

Trout have comparatively soft mouths, so you do not have to set the hook hard. The fine-wire hooks on most flies and trout lures penetrate easily, assuming they're well-sharpened. Fly fishermen often make the mistake of jerking the rod too hard when a trout takes the fly, snapping the light tippet.

When you hook a trout, it usually makes a powerful initial run. Unless the fish heads for snaggy cover, don't try to stop it. With spinning tackle, make sure your drag is set on the light side. With a fly rod, let the reel handle spin freely; the clicker will prevent the line from overrunning. When you hook a large trout or salmon, it's a good idea to slow the run as soon as possible so the fish can't reach the rapids and swim into the next pool.

You may have to follow the fish if it takes too much line. After the initial run, start applying some pressure. Keep your rod tip high enough for the rod to absorb the force of a sudden run. If the fish jumps, quickly lower your rod tip to reduce the tension. Otherwise, a head shake could break your line. Don't let the fish rest; it will soon tire if you maintain steady pressure.

Small trout hooked on a fly rod can be landed by simply stripping in line, but with bigger trout it pays to use your reel so you have the advantage of a mechanical drag.

If possible, when fly fishing keep the entire leader outside the tip-top during the fight. The line-to-leader connection could hang up in the guides should a trout make a last-minute run, and the tippet could snap. Using a needle knot rather than a nail knot will minimize the problem.

When you plan to release the fish, play it as quickly as possible. If the fight drags on, the fish may become too stressed to survive. A light tippet, while considered very sporting, results in a longer fight that may kill the trout. Even if it swims away, it may die later.

Net the fish, or beach it if you're near a gradually sloping bank. When you lead a trout into the shallows and it feels bottom, it often panics and beaches itself.

TIPS FOR HOOKING, PLAYING, & LANDING TROUT ON FLIES

Wait until the trout sucks in a dry fly and closes its mouth before setting the hook. If you try to set too soon, you'll pull the fly out of its mouth.

Palm the spool of an exposed-rim fly reel for extra drag. This keeps a big steelhead or salmon from getting into a rapids and running too far downstream.

Set the hook by lifting the rod with a stiff wrist while stripping in line with your other hand. Lift the rod tip straight up rather than pulling back.

Keep your net out of the water while the trout is still "green." Putting the net into the water before the fish tires may cause it to dart away.

Net the trout headfirst when it tires, plunging the net under it quickly. To keep the fish from breaking off in the net, slacken the line as you lift.

Avoid chasing the trout with your net. If you attempt to net the trout tail-first, it may feel the net and surge forward, breaking your line.

TIPS TO MINIMIZE SPOOKING

You can minimize spooking by following these guidelines:

- Keep a low profile; the lower you are, the less likely you will appear in the trout's window of vision. To fish a narrow stream, you may have to crawl to the bank and cast from a kneeling position.

- Wear drab clothing that blends in with the surroundings. A bright-colored shirt or cap can put the trout down in a hurry.

- In turbulent water, you can approach a trout more closely than in slow or slack water.

- Use objects such as boulders and trees to conceal your approach. If there is no place to hide, try to stay in the shadows.

- When you reach a likely spot, stand still for a few minutes before making a cast. When you first arrive, trout detect your presence and stop feeding. After a few minutes, they may get used to you and start to feed again, even if you are plainly visible.

- Try to avoid casting over the trout's window of vision, especially with bright-colored fly line.

CATCH-AND-RELEASE

Production of trout can be measured like production of crops. Just as farmers record crop yields in bushels per acre (0.4 ha), fisheries managers record trout yields in pounds (kg) per acre (0.4 ha).

Hat Creek, a heavily fished California stream, produces about 60 pounds (27.3 kg) of trout per acre (0.4 ha) per year. In 1983, a creel census was conducted on a 3½-mile (5.6 km) stretch of the stream, which had a total annual production estimated at 2800 pounds (1272.7 kg) of trout. In that year, over 20,000 pounds (9,090.9 kg) of trout were caught, over seven times the productive capacity of the stream. Fortunately, most of these fish were released. It's obvious that this stream could not continue to provide good fishing for the entire season unless anglers returned a good share of their trout to the water.

Heavy fishing pressure on some popular streams has prompted conservation agencies to enact catch-and-release regulations. And even where such regulations are not in effect, more and more anglers are voluntarily returning most of their trout.

There's no disputing the concept of catch-and-release fishing, but unless anglers know exactly how to release their fish, many will die from mishandling. If you follow the procedure shown on the next page, the trout and salmon you release will have an excellent chance of survival.

Flatten your barbs so you can remove hooks without injuring the fish. By keeping a tight line during the fight, you will seldom lose a fish.

Move to a location out of the current to play the fish. This way, it cannot use the current to its advantage, so it tires more quickly.

Leave the fish in the water, grasp the hook with a pliers or hemostat, then gently shake the hook to release the fish. This way, you won't remove the protective slime.

Cut the leader if a fish is deeply hooked. In a Wisconsin study, 56 percent of deep-hooked trout survived when the leader was cut; 11 percent when the hook was removed.

Hold the fish in an upright position facing into the current. Give it time to recover so it can swim away on its own. If it starts to sink, hold it upright a while longer.

Avoid landing salmon with a tailer. When the noose tightens around the tail, protective film and tissue are removed, making the fish susceptible to infection.

FISHING FOR TROPHY TROUT

An average stream angler seldom catches a big trout. The trophy angler catches considerably fewer trout, but the challenge of outwitting a big one makes up for the lack of quantity. To improve the chances of taking a trophy, the trophy angler fishes in different places and uses different techniques than other anglers.

Look for big trout in the deepest pools or undercuts, or at least in areas where they can easily reach a deep-water retreat. Just how deep is relative. In a small creek, a 4-foot (1.2 m) pool is deep enough to hold a big one. In a large river, an 8-foot (2.4 m) pool may not be deep enough.

Big trout prey on smaller ones, so when a likely looking pool fails to produce even a small trout, this may be a clue that the pool is home to an exceptionally large trout. It pays to try such a pool from time to time rather than giving up on it.

Of course, some streams are more likely to produce big trout than others. Tailwater streams, coastal streams, and streams connected to large lakes generally yield the biggest trout.

A trophy trout is more likely to be near the bottom than is a small trout, so sinking flies or deep-running lures are usually more effective than dry flies or shallow-runners.

Because fish make up a greater percentage of a trout's diet as it grows older, fish-imitating lures like minnow plugs, spinners, and streamers take larger trout than do small, insect-imitating flies. Some trophy hunters use streamers that measure up to 4 inches (10.2 cm).

Big dry flies can be deadly during a hatch of large insects. In the northern Rockies, trophy-class trout that normally ignore insects go on a feeding rampage when large stoneflies, known as salmon flies, are hatching. On many eastern streams, big trout gorge themselves during the green drake mayfly hatch.

A hefty trout does not like to exert itself too much. Rather than racing smaller trout to catch fast-moving foods, it lies in wait for the chance to grab unsuspecting prey. Regardless of the type of bait or lure, a slow presentation generally works best.

Any type of trout fishing requires an inconspicuous approach to avoid putting the fish down. However, when you're after trophies, stealth is even more important. The reason these trout have grown so large is that they have learned to sense predators, including anglers. Some trophy specialists go to extremes to avoid detection; they cast from behind bushes, or stay upstream of the pool and let the current carry their bait to the fish. For trophy browns, serious anglers do almost all their fishing at night.

WHERE TO FIND TROPHY TROUT

Hard-to-reach pockets, like a deep hole beneath roots or branches, often hold big trout. Most anglers shy away from such spots because of snags.

Downstream reaches that would seem too warm and muddy for trout usually have high baitfish populations that attract trophy browns.

Remote stream stretches or those where brushy banks restrict access usually hold bigger trout than easily accessible stretches.

Chapter 4
FLY FISHING FOR TROUT & SALMON

Why fly fish? After all, you can catch trout and salmon by spinning or baitcasting, both of which are easier to learn.

Fly fishing is by far the oldest of these methods, with a history stretching back centuries. So the modern fly angler, equipped with a lightweight graphite rod rather than a buggy-whip wooden pole, has the satisfaction of carrying on a long and colorful tradition.

But nostalgia, no matter how strong, can't account for the survival of this age-old method into the space age, or for the manifold increase in its popularity in recent years. Despite its ancient origins, fly fishing remains a versatile and productive way to outwit wary salmonids.

Many of the most common foods for trout can be imitated only with flies; even the tiniest spinning and casting lures are much too bulky. Aquatic insects, such as mayflies and caddisflies, make up most of the diet of stream trout. Imitations of these delicate creatures are much too light to be cast with ordinary spinning or baitcasting techniques.

In fact, flies can successfully imitate any trout food. With a 6- or 7-weight fly line and a rod to match, you can fish with anything from the tiniest midge imitations, not much bigger than a gnat, on up to streamers that simulate minnows several inches (cm) long.

The most frantic and exciting angling for stream trout comes during cloudlike insect hatches. Yet it can also be the most frustrating. The fish may be rising all around you, but if you're limited to casting hardware, you're almost certainly out of luck. When rising to a hatch, trout generally refuse all imitations of other types of food.

Some of the biggest trout feed almost entirely on baitfish. In lakes, spoons and minnow plugs usually work better for these fish than streamer flies, which don't have much action in the still water. In streams, though, the current gives streamers an erratic, undulating movement more lifelike than the steady wobbling of hardware. Generally, you can mimic the size, shape, and color of particular baitfish more closely with flies than with plugs or spoons.

Many famous trout streams have fly-fishing-only regulations. These regulations are designed to reduce hooking mortality and ensure a healthy population of trout for everyone who wants to catch fish. Even on streams that allow spinning and baitcasting equipment, such tackle makes it difficult to present a fly realistically enough for the educated trout found in these waters. For casting flies softly and maneuvering them like living creatures through a maze of current, fly fishing tackle nearly always works best.

It's true that learning to fly fish takes time and effort. To become really skilled may require several seasons of experience on the water. It's also true that you can start enjoying this traditional way of angling, and start catching fish, after only a couple brief practice sessions.

As in any other kind of fishing, the learning is part of the fun. Actually, it's a process that never ends, even if you fish a lifetime. The tips on the following pages will get you started right.

RIGGING UP

When trout are rising but won't take a fly, you may wonder if you're using the wrong pattern or perhaps the wrong size. And if you hook a fish but fail to catch it, you may ponder what mistake you made while fighting it. In both cases, however, you might be asking yourself the wrong questions.

Many costly errors in fly fishing are made even before the first cast. To present the fly realistically and to hold a running or jumping fish, you must rig your tackle carefully. It's tempting to rush the preliminaries, especially when you arrive at the stream and a hatch is already under way. Fly tackle takes longer to rig than other kinds of equipment, but experienced anglers know it's time well spent.

Do as much of the rigging as possible before you leave home. Tie a length of heavy monofilament to the tip of your fly line with a needle knot. For lines up to 4-weight, use 0.017-inch mono (0.043 cm); for 5- to 7-weight lines, 0.019-inch (0.048 cm); for 8-weight and heavier, 0.021-inch (0.053 cm). In the other end of the mono, tie a perfection loop. When finished, this mono connector should be 4 to 6 inches (10.2 to 15.2 cm) long.

Tie another perfection loop in the end of your leader butt. This loop will join to the one on the connector, making leader changes quick and simple.

Use blood knots to join a tippet to a knotless leader, and to join various sections of a knotted leader.

On the stream, thread the leader through the rod guides, and then take a minute or two to straighten it. Pull a short section repeatedly between your fingers; the stretching and heat from the friction will remove the coils. Continue until the entire leader is straight. Otherwise, it won't unroll properly on the cast, and when you fish with subsurface flies the springy mono will keep you from detecting strikes.

Instead of straightening the leader with bare fingers, you can use a leader straightener. Then you can pull harder without cutting or burning your skin.

Always check the sharpness of your hook. Try running the point across a fingernail; it will catch in the nail if well sharpened. Dull hooks should be touched up with a hone. Make sure the point hasn't been damaged by snagging on rocks. If it's bent slightly you can usually straighten it carefully with a small pair of needle-nose pliers. But if any of the point is broken off, discard the fly. Many anglers flatten the barbs

TYING LOOPS IN LEADER BUTT & MONO CONNECTOR

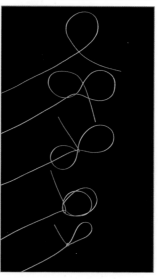

Perfection loop. (top to bottom) Make a loop by passing the free end under the standing line. Wrap the free end around, to form a second loop on top of the first. Wrap the free end around once more, passing it between the loops. Pass the top loop through the bottom one. Tighten and trim.

LOOP-TO-LOOP CONNECTION

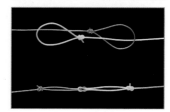

Loop connection. (top) Pass the leader-butt loop through the loop in the fly-line connector, then run all the leader through the butt loop. (bottom) Snug.

on their fly hooks for easier penetration, and for quicker removal with no injury to the fish.

For tying subsurface flies to your tippet, the best knot is a Duncan loop. A loop knot allows the fly to swing naturally in the current, but you can sometimes get by with a knot that draws tight on the hook eye. The Duncan loop is stronger than other loop knots, but it may tighten on the eye under the pressure of a snag or a large fish. With your fingernails, you can usually slide the knot back up the line to reopen the loop.

Tie dry flies on with a clinch knot. When tightening, make certain to center the knot at the front of the hook eye, with the line pointing straight ahead or slightly downward. This ensures the fly will float in the most natural attitude.

TYING TIPPET TO LEADER	TYING SUBSURFACE FLIES TO TIPPET	TYING DRY FLIES TO TIPPET

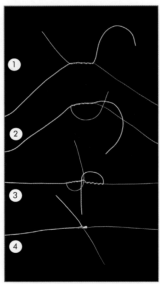 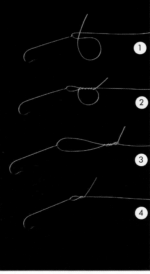 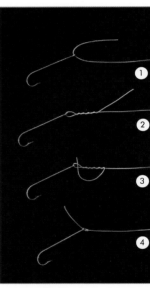

Blood knot. (1) Cross the two sections of mono. (2) With one of the ends, make four turns around the other section. (3) Bring the end back around between the two lines. (4) Repeat with the other end, inserting it in the opening so it points opposite the first end. (5) Wet the knot, then pull on the standing ends to tighten. Trim close.

Duncan loop knot. (1) Thread the tippet through the hook eye, then form a loop next to the standing line. (2) Make four to six turns around one side of the loop and the standing line. Wet the knot and (3) tighten it by pulling on the fly and the free end, then on the fly and the standing line. (4) Slide the tightened knot within 1/8 to 1/4 inch (0.32 to 0.64 cm) of the hook eye, and pull hard on the free end with needle-nose pliers to secure it there. Trim.

Double clinch knot. (1) Pass end of tippet through hook eye. (2) Wind tag end around standing line 3 1/4 to 8 times, depending on tippet diameter. (3) Bring tag end back through loop nearest hook eye. (4) Pull standing line until knot is snug against hook eye. Trim tag.

CASTING A FLY

Fly casting differs from other methods of casting in several important respects:

- Because a fly weighs so little, you cast the weight of the fly line itself, which is thicker and heavier than other kinds of line.

- Each casting stroke, forward or back, consists of two movements blended together. Using your forearm, you load the rod, raising the tip to start the line moving and to put a deep bend in the rod. You finish the stroke with a wrist snap, with a sudden application of force as in spinning. The keys to smooth fly casting are the proper timing and gradual acceleration of each stroke, not a sudden application of force as in spinning.

Gradual acceleration ensures that the line will flow out straight on the cast. If you apply too much power too soon, the rod tip will bounce at the end of the stroke, throwing waves of slack into the line. On the following stroke, this slack will make it impossible to load the rod.

The loop formed in your line as it travels forward or rearward should be narrow, no more than 2 feet (60 cm) in width. A narrow loop has little air resistance, so your line travels fast without sagging to the water, and has less chance of blowing off target.

Before attempting to fish, spend some time practicing on water or an open lawn. Any balanced trout outfit will do, but a 6-weight rod with a weight-forward floating line is ideal. Tie on a leader 7½ feet (2.3 m) long and a piece of bright yarn to simulate the fly.

Start by learning the basic overhead cast. Once you have it mastered, practice false casting, shooting line, and roll casting. Then you'll be ready to catch trout. The double haul is an advanced technique for distance casting, which you can learn later on. Usually, the most effective range for trout is just 25 to 40 feet (7.6 to 12.2 m).

HOW TO MAKE THE BASIC OVERHEAD CAST

Begin by letting out the desired amount of line in front of you. Stand facing the target with your feet spread comfortably apart. Position your rod hand so the tip of the rod is pointing in the direction of your target, with your rod, forearm, and wrist aligned. Lower your rod tip and remove the slack from the line.

Raise your rod and begin to accelerate slowly and continuously until the entire fly line is off the water.

Apply a short backward speed stroke, forcing a bend in the rod and generating the energy necessary to propel the line into the back cast.

Stop the rod crisply. A loop will form in the line as it moves overhead. The shorter the speed stroke and straighter the casting plane, the tighter the loop will be.

Pause as the back cast unrolls behind you. When the line unrolls to only a small "J" in the air, begin your forward acceleration. Apply a short forward speed stroke and immediately stop the rod. Aim your cast about eye level above your target. Let the line settle to the water while lowering the rod tip to the fishing position.

False Casting

The false cast is a necessary supplement to the basic overhead cast. Instead of letting your line and fly settle to the water on the forward cast, you keep them in the air and make another back cast. False casting serves several purposes:

- You can cancel an off-target cast; just pull into a back cast and correct your aim on the next cast forward.

- You can change directions from one cast to the next. It's difficult to pick your line off the water, make a single back cast, and aim the forward cast at a target off to your side. Instead, you false cast once in an intermediate direction and then hit the target on the next cast.

- In fishing with dry flies, a succession of false casts helps air-dry the hackle so the fly floats high and keeps its natural appearance.

- For additional distance, shoot line on a false cast. Generally, the more line you strip in on the retrieve, the more false casts it will take to cast the same distance again.

HOW TO FALSE CAST

Lift line off water as you would on a normal overhead cast.

Let the back cast unroll behind you until the line forms a small "J."

Aim your forward cast higher than you would on an overhead cast. Do not allow the line to settle on the water. Instead, wait until the small "J" forms in the line and begin another back cast. Repeat as necessary.

Shooting Line

Usually you want to cast more line than you pick up from the water. If your previous cast was 40 feet (12.2 m) long and you retrieved 15 feet (4.6 m) while fishing the fly, you need to shoot line if you want to reach out more than the 25 feet (7.6 m) you picked up. To do so, you simply release line while the loop is in the air; the unrolling line pulls more out behind it.

Before starting a cast, make sure you have enough running line stripped off the reel. Let it lie on the water, or hold it in loose coils with your line hand. You can shoot line on a forward cast or on a back cast.

Shoot line by forming a large "O" with your thumb and forefinger immediately after the wrist snap on the cast. Allow loose line to flow, or shoot, through it.

How to Roll Cast

When obstructions prevent a normal back cast, use the roll cast. With this technique you cannot reach out as far as with a normal cast; the maximum distance is about 40 feet (12.2 m). Roll casting must be practiced on water, not land. A double-taper line works best; with a weight-forward, the running line is too light to pick up the belly.

Ease your rod tip rearward and tilt it away from you, so the line hangs outside the rod and slightly behind it. Then pause until the line stops moving.

Move your arm forward and downward smoothly, then accelerate quickly and make a forward speed stroke, and stop the rod crisply. The line will roll toward the target in a wide loop and straighten.

The Double Haul

Long casts are often necessary in salmon and steelhead fishing, and occasionally in other types of trout fishing. The double haul increases line speed on the back cast and again on the forward cast, so you can make long casts and punch into the wind. This technique can increase your casting distance by 50 percent.

Make a short, smooth downward tug, or haul, about 4 to 6 inches (10 to 15 cm), during the acceleration phase of the back cast.

Bring your hand back up immediately after the haul. Let the line unroll behind you as you would on a normal overhead cast.

Make a second haul, equal in length to the first, during the acceleration phase of the forward cast.

Bring your line hand back up immediately after the haul. If you are shooting line, form an "O" with the fingers of your line hand instead.

COMMON MISTAKES IN FLY CASTING

Starting the back cast with the rod pointed high allows slack line to sag from the rod tip. With the slack, you cannot fully load the rod.

Turning the arm or wrist so the reel aims outward waves the rod in a semicircle, widening line loops. The rod must go straight back and forward.

FISHING WITH DRY FLIES

Nothing is more suspenseful than watching a big trout or salmon rise slowly to a floating fly, perhaps to reject it at the last moment, or perhaps to engulf it and give you a battle demanding all your finesse.

Despite the intimidating technical discussions in books and magazines, dry-fly angling is generally the easiest way to fool a trout with a fly. It offers these advantages:

- You can read surface currents easily.

- If the trout are rising, you can see where they are and often what they're feeding on.

- You know exactly where your fly is and whether it's working as it should.

- You can detect strikes by sight.

Dry flies are designed to imitate the adult stages of various aquatic insects. The classic dry, with a stiff tail and hackle and a pair of upright wings, is a good approximation of a mayfly. Stonefly imitations are similar but larger, with a single hair wing angled backward. Caddis patterns are small, like mayfly imitations, but have wings lying tentlike along the body; they are sometimes tied without hackle. Midge flies, almost microscopic, have hackle but no wings.

When selecting a dry fly on the stream, most anglers attempt to match the hatch. Recognize, however, that trout often feed selectively, and the particular insects you notice first, the biggest or most abundant species, may not be the ones they want. Examine the rises and the naturals adrift on the stream to determine what the fish actually are taking. If you don't have a fly that duplicates them in size, shape, and color, settle for matching just the size. An artificial slightly smaller than the real thing usually works better than one that's bigger.

Traditionally, dry-fly anglers have fished in an upstream direction. The fly drifts toward you, so you strip in line and can easily pick up the short length remaining on the water when you're ready for the next cast. Cast diagonally upstream, rather than straight up, so your leader and line won't drift over the fish and spook it. To reach difficult lies, you may want to cast across stream or downstream.

Regardless of the direction you cast, always drop your fly well upstream of the fish and let it drift into position. Remember, the rises of a fish are misleading; they do not indicate the spot where the trout actually lies.

On a drift, you must avoid drag. If the current pulls your line so the fly is dragged across the surface, the trout will refuse it and may even stop rising. Keep some slack in your leader at all times, and in your line, if needed. Once the line is on the water, you can mend it to maintain slack. When you fish in a downstream direction, simply pay out your line as fast as the current takes it.

At times, the drag-free drift may be less productive than skating a dry fly across the surface. You do this by making a short cast downstream, then holding your rod tip high and shaking it gently from side to side while stripping in line. The fly will skip erratically on the water, like a caddisfly attempting flight. The action is very different from the steady slide across the surface resulting from drag.

Dry flies often catch trout and salmon when they aren't rising, and even when no insects are hatching at all. Under these conditions, you drift your fly naturally to the spots where fish are most likely to lie, or skate it over them. An effective tactic is to make several casts to a single spot, creating the illusion of a hatch.

Dry flies are used in sizes 8 to 28 for most trout, and sizes 2 to 8 for steelhead and Atlantic salmon.

How to Fish Across Stream with the Reach Cast

This cast puts a wide upstream curve of slack in your line, doubling the length of your drift before a downstream curve, or belly, forms in the line and drag sets in. You can make a backhand reach cast or a forehand, depending on the direction of the current.

Make a normal forward cast, allowing some line to shoot through the guides as the loop starts to unroll toward the target.

Point your rod tip as far as possible to the side from which the current is flowing. Continue to shoot line while moving your rod to the side.

Stop the line when your fly is over the target. The line falls well upstream of the fly, so you won't have to mend so soon.

How to Fish Downstream with the S-Cast

When you fish downstream, the S-cast will put slack in your entire line, giving you a long drag-free drift. A lot of narrow S-curves work better than a few wide ones; wide curves reduce casting accuracy and are difficult to pick up from the water when you set the hook.

Direct the cast well above the water, shooting line. Use just enough power to reach the target, so you don't have to brake the cast.

Shake the rod rapidly from side to side, forming curves in the line. The line must continue to shoot, or the curves will straighten.

Bring the rod tip down as the line settles. The fly will drift freely until the curves wash out. You can extend the drift by paying out line.

FISHING WITH WET FLIES

The standard wet fly has almost become a museum piece. A century ago, it was the only artificial fly in use in America; today the angler who wants a sunken fly is far more likely to tie on a streamer or nymph, which more closely resembles important trout food such as baitfish and larval insects.

Traditional wet-fly techniques are the simplest and most effortless in fly fishing. There's less casting than with dry flies, so you cover the water more quickly. Also, wets are effective in fast, broken currents that would quickly drown any dry. Wet flies are generally much smaller and less air-resistant than streamers, so they're easier to cast. In addition, your presentation and retrieve need not be as precise as in fishing with nymphs.

Wet flies have soft, absorbent hackle for quick sinking and lifelike action. The standard wet has a feather wing; dull-tinted patterns of this type are thought to represent drowned adult insects. Feather-wing wets with gaudy colors and metallic tinsels may suggest tiny baitfish, but serve mainly as attractors useful for brook trout and Atlantic salmon. Some wet patterns, called hackle flies, lack wings; these may resemble insect larvae or leeches.

The most popular wet flies today are specialized types. Large patterns with wings of hair or marabou, often in bright attractor colors, are commonly used for steelhead and salmon. Fat-bodied hackle flies called wooly worms, which have hackle along their entire length, are favorites for trout of all kinds on big western rivers.

Wet flies are often drifted at random, covering lots of potential holding water rather than particular lies. The wet-fly drift technique, with a floating or sink tip line, works especially well in long runs and riffles that lack large boulders or other obvious cover. In such places, trout take shelter near small obstructions or in depressions in the bottom that may be invisible from the surface.

You can also fish specific targets. Cast across the stream and let your fly drift into the calm pockets around logs, rocks, and other objects. When it reaches a pocket, feed line into the current—the fly stays where it is, but the belly expands downstream. Otherwise, the current would sweep the fly away immediately.

In fall and winter steelheading, it's usually necessary to fish wet flies very deep. Use the wet-fly drift with a fast-sinking shooting head or a lead-core head. Many wet flies designed for steelhead have weighted bodies or bead heads; they will bounce along the bottom without snagging if the rocks are rounded.

Wet flies are used in sizes 10 to 18 for most trout, and sizes 2 to 8 for steelhead and salmon.

HOW TO FISH WITH THE WET-FLY DRIFT

Make a short cast across the current. In swift water, cast slightly downstream to minimize the belly and keep the line from being pulled downstream too quickly. In slower current, cast slightly upstream, so more belly will form and speed up the fly.

Mend your line to control the speed of your fly. If the fly swings too slowly, make a downstream mend (shown) to increase belly and accelerate the fly. If your fly swings too quickly, throw an upstream mend to reduce the belly and slow the fly.

Let the fly swing until it hangs in the current below you and begins to rise. You'll get a high percentage of your strikes at this point.

Lengthen each subsequent cast by 1 to 3 feet (0.3 to 0.9 m) until you've covered all the water you can reach. Then, take a step or two downstream and repeat the process.

FISHING WITH NYMPHS

Day in and day out, the odds favor the fly angler who uses a nymph. No matter how low or high the stream may be, no matter how cold or warm the weather, the naturals that nymphs imitate are always present and available to the trout.

Nymphs are intended to copy the immature forms of aquatic insects, including mayflies, stoneflies, caddisflies, dragonflies, damselflies, and midges. Some nymphs are close imitations of particular species, as exact as fly tiers can make them. Others are impressionistic, meant to suggest a variety of naturals in form, size, and coloration. Many nymphs of both these types have bodies that are thick at the front and thinner at the rear, simulating the wing pads and abdomens of the real thing. Usually, there's a soft, sparse hackle to serve as legs.

A nymph pattern may be tied in weighted and unweighted versions. Weighted nymphs have lead or copper wire wound onto the hook shank under the body material. They are used for fishing near the bottom, especially in fast currents. Unweighted nymphs work well for fishing shallow; because they have livelier action, many experts prefer them for fishing deep in slow water as well. To carry them deep, attach split shot or lead wrap to the leader. A few nymphs are designed to float, imitating the immature insect at the moment it arrives on the surface to transform into an adult.

No one becomes a complete nymph fisherman overnight. Techniques for fishing nymphs are far more numerous and varied than those for any other type of fly. Some are simple, but others are the most challenging of all ways of catching trout.

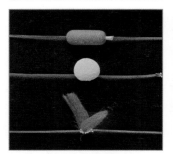

Popular strike indicators include: (top to bottom) Styrofoam float pegged in place with a toothpick; Adhesive foam, which pinches onto your leader and sticks in place; and colored yarn tied into a blood knot in your leader.

Depending on species and stage of life, the naturals may crawl across the bottom, burrow in it, swim, or simply tumble along with the current. Thus, the nymph fisherman can work his fly realistically by drifting it freely with the current, or by twitching or stripping it along at various depths.

Detecting strikes in nymph fishing can be difficult. When you use a natural drift, it's generally impossible to feel the hit. The best solution is to use a floating line with a bright-colored tip, a leader with a fluorescent butt, or some kind of strike indicator (see photo) attached to the leader. If you see any twitch or hesitation, set the hook.

For greatest sensitivity, strike indicators should be positioned as close to the fly as possible. To fish shallow, place the indicator just above the tippet knot. To fish deep, move it back toward the leader butt.

Keep your casts short so you can see the twitch more clearly. If you use a sink tip line, keep an eye on the point where the lighter-colored floating portion appears below the surface.

One of the easiest nymph techniques, and one of the most effective, is the wet-fly drift. It's a good way to fish runs and riffles that lack obvious cover to cast to. By planning a drift carefully, you can also use this technique to swing your fly close to boulders or logs, or to nymphing trout you can actually see.

Sometimes these nymphing fish are visible only as flashes near the streambed, as they turn and dart in the current to feed. At other times, their tails make swirls on the surface when they tip nose down to take nymphs on the bottom, or their backs may break water when they feed on naturals that are only a few inches deep. Anglers often mistake these swirls for rises to adult insects, and make futile attempts to catch the trout with dry flies.

When drifting a nymph to a feeding fish, try to sink it exactly to the fish's eye level. To increase the depth of a drift, angle your cast farther upstream so the fly will have more time to sink before reaching the trout. Use a weighted nymph if necessary, or add a suitable amount of weight to your leader.

In the still water of pools, try making a long cast, letting the nymph sink near the bottom, then retrieving it in short twitches. In very cold water, especially in the early season, a nymph allowed to lie motionless on the bottom and twitched only occasionally may be more effective than anything else except live bait. Stay alert for strikes; a trout may pick up the loitering nymph and drop it instantly.

Nymphs used for trout range from size 1/0 to 18.

HOW TO FISH A NYMPH UPSTREAM

Make a short cast upstream, so your nymph will drift to a visible fish or probable lie. If possible, cast at an angle rather than straight upstream, so your line won't drift over the fish and spook it.

Strip line in as the current carries the nymph toward you. Let the fly drift naturally; to prevent drag, your line should have slight curves of slack. Twitch the fly when it reaches the fish or the lie.

Watch your strike indicator closely. If it flicks or pauses at any time during the drift, set the hook instantly. Too long a delay, or too much slack in the drifting line, will cause you to miss the strike.

HOW TO FISH A CURRENT EDGE WITH A DOWNSTREAM MEND

Angle your cast upstream into the edge of a fast current. Trout will hold in the slower water near shore, watching for nymphs to wash down in the fast current, and darting out to grab them.

Mend your line by flipping a curve of slack downstream. Because the tip of the line is in the faster water, a belly forms upstream, the reverse of the usual situation. Without a mend, the fly would drift slower than the current.

FISHING WITH STREAMERS

If you're serious about catching big trout, try fishing with streamers. The real heavyweights feed almost exclusively on baitfish; most streamers are tied to mimic shiners, dace, sculpins, chubs, darters, and even young trout.

Not that streamers are invariably the flies to select. When the water conditions are ideal for feeding, trout show more interest in dries, nymphs, and wets. Streamers produce most dependably when dries and wets don't, such as during periods when the water is very cold or discolored.

Pick the right times, and you may come up with a trophy. Not only do streamers attract the attention of big trout better than small flies, they also give you a better chance of hanging on once a fish is hooked. The big, stout hooks hold securely, and the heavy tippets generally used with streamers make break-offs less likely.

The traditional streamer has a wing of long hackle feathers, but other types are more popular today. Patterns with hair wings are often called bucktails, even if the hair is synthetic or comes from animals other than deer. Another type, the Zonker, has a strip of soft fur tied along the top of the hook. Muddlers have large heads, usually of clipped deer hair, to simulate the outline of sculpins.

Some brightly colored streamers do not closely imitate any baitfish, but instead work as attractors. Often, these bright flies draw more strikes than realistic ones. Or, trout may swirl at an attractor pattern, revealing their whereabouts, but refuse to take it. Then you can switch to a realistic streamer or some other type of fly more likely to draw a strike.

Because of their size and bulk, streamers produce more vibration than other flies when stripped through the water. This extra attraction helps fish locate them in roily water or after dark. Muddler and diver patterns, with their oversize heads, make the most underwater disturbance.

Like nymphs, streamers are tied with or without built-in weight, and may be fished with floating or sink tip lines, or with sinking shooting heads. Split shot or other weight may be added to the leader as needed.

The wet-fly drift is a good basic technique for streamers. You can twitch the fly during the drift for a more convincing minnow-like action. Mend the line often, so the fly does not speed unnaturally through the current. Proper mending also keeps the streamer drifting broadside to the current, so it's more visible to fish lying in wait.

In slower current that does not give the fly much action, you can cast across stream, then strip the fly back toward you as it slowly swings downstream. No mending is needed, since the fly is retrieved before a wide belly can develop. The streamer simulates a baitfish darting across the current. Even when conditions are not ideal for streamers, this technique enables you to cover water very quickly, tempting trout to swirl at the fly as they would at an attractor pattern.

Streamers are used in sizes 1/0 to 10 for trout, sizes 1/0 to 4 for salmon.

HOW TO FISH A MUDDLER ON THE SURFACE

Twitch a muddler across flat water, pausing occasionally, to imitate a grasshopper or struggling baitfish. Work the fly close to grassy banks, especially near undercuts. The head and hair collar behind it should be dressed with floatant.

HOW TO HANG A STREAMER IN THE CURRENT

Swing your streamer near a boulder or log. Let it hang there a minute or so, waving in the current; twitch it occasionally. This works well for steelhead and salmon, which often strike only if given a long look at the fly.

Keep a foot (30 cm) of slack line between the reel and your finger when hanging a streamer in current. On a strike, you can instantly release this slack to soften the shock to the tippet.

FISHING WITH SPECIAL PURPOSE FLIES

Historically, almost all flies were tied to imitate insects or baitfish. However, anglers have come to realize that fish aren't always interested in such offerings. At times, other foods are more abundant and the trout prefer them to the everyday fare.

Certain of these morsels, such as leeches, crayfish, and salmon eggs, seem to defy imitation with fur and feathers. Still, imaginative fly tiers have come up with realistic copies, and inventive anglers have devised techniques to bring them to life.

The most popular of these special purpose flies are terrestrials. These simulate land insects such as ants, grasshoppers, crickets, beetles, and inchworms, any of which may fall onto the water. Terrestrial flies are effective throughout the warm months. They're especially useful in late summer, when aquatic hatches wane. Terrestrials are fished on the surface in slow to moderate current, where the surface is relatively smooth.

Ant imitations often work better than standard dry flies on days when no trout are rising. Floating ants in sizes 18 to 22 are drifted close to the banks, where natural ants are most likely to be. These tiny flies are difficult to see, so keep your casts short, and strike gently at any rise near your fly. Sinking ants are usually tied in sizes 8 to 20. Drift ant imitations with a floating line, mending often to avoid drag.

Grasshopper patterns, in sizes 4 to 14, are most productive in meadow streams, particularly on windy days when the naturals are blown onto the water. Dead drift them along grassy banks, adding an occasional twitch. Beetles and jassids (small flat-bodied insects, also known as leafhoppers) are inconspicuous on the water, but in warm weather the trout may feed on them selectively. Beetle imitations are tied in sizes 10 to 20; jassids, sizes 16 to 22. A dead drift on the surface works best.

Leech flies are among the top lures for big trout. These are big flies, size 2 to 10. The dressings, in most cases, consist mainly of marabou or rabbit fur. These soft materials have an undulating action that matches the squirming of the naturals. Work leech flies in slow current with the wet-fly drift, twitching them from time to time. In still water, retrieve with long, slow strips; a jerky action would make the fur or marabou flare out from the hook, spoiling the illusion of a real leech.

Scud patterns imitate tiny crustaceans that are superabundant in many trout streams, especially spring creeks. Trout often gorge themselves on scuds, burrowing into weedbeds and rooting them out. It's not unusual to catch a trout that is so stuffed with scuds that it regurgitates them when you attempt to unhook it. When trout gorge themselves this heavily, they're tough to catch, but you may be able to draw a strike by drifting a scud pattern so it nearly hits the fish on the nose. Scud flies range from size 10 to 20.

It's not unusual in spring creeks to catch a trout that's gorged on tiny crustaceans, called scuds.

Crayfish flies should be worked close to rocky streambeds, either drifting them with the current or stripping them briskly through quiet water. Crayfish are most plentiful in limestone streams, and become most active in low light. A good time to fish the imitations, in sizes 1/0 to 8, is at dusk or after dark.

In streams with runs of Pacific salmon, other salmonids like rainbows, Dolly Varden, and grayling feed heavily on salmon eggs. Fly anglers take trophy fish by dead-drifting egg flies in fluorescent red, pink, or orange. Use just enough weight on your leader to reach bottom; big trout may drop the fly immediately if they feel resistance. Egg patterns also are tied in white and chartreuse to imitate the spawn of suckers and other fishes.

Chapter 5
SPINNING & BAITCASTING TECHNIQUES

For the average angler, spinning and baitcasting are much easier than fly fishing. Plus, in some situations, they catch more and bigger trout. Because trout eat more baitfish and fewer insects as they grow larger, good-sized baits and lures have more appeal than small flies.

The monofilament line used with spinning and baitcasting gear offers several advantages to stream anglers. The small diameter line cuts the current much better than fly line, so drag is not as much of a problem, and you can fish deep more easily. Mono is also less wind-resistant, which makes casting in a headwind or crosswind considerably easier. Fly line is highly visible; if you cast over a trout, or allow your line to drift ahead of the fly, the fish may spook. With mono, your presentation need not be as precise.

When heavy rains cloud a stream, fly fishing may be tough, but spinfishers and baitcasters continue catching trout. The fish can still detect the scent of natural bait or the sound and vibration of plugs and spinners.

On a narrow, brushy stream, fly casting is almost impossible because streamside obstacles foul your back cast. But with a short, ultralight spinning outfit, you can flip small lures beneath overhanging branches and into fish pockets that otherwise would be difficult to reach. Spinning gear is also an advantage on wide streams because you can make long casts and cover a lot of water in a hurry.

Baitcasting gear is the best choice for exceptionally large trout and salmon. The level-wind reel eliminates the line twist problems that plague spinfishers when big fish strip line from their reels.

JIG FISHING

Until recently, jigs were reserved for warmwater species like bass and walleyes. Few anglers even considered using them for trout. Yet jigs do have a place in trout fishing, and in the hands of an expert they can be deadly. Even fly anglers are discovering the effectiveness of nymphs tied on tiny jig hooks.

Jigs resemble favorite trout foods such as minnows, insect larvae, crustaceans, leeches, and salmon eggs. Try to match your jig color to the fish's natural food. A black or brown jig, for instance, would be a good match for most insect larvae; an orange jig, for salmon eggs.

When trout are aggressive, a jig with a tail dressing of soft plastic, marabou, or hair is all you need. When trout are fussy, try tipping your jig with some type of natural bait, like a piece of worm or a small minnow.

Jigs work as well for small trout as for larger trout and salmon. They cast easily and sink rapidly in the current. A jig of the proper weight hugs the bottom and is not swept by the current as much as most other lures. And, jigs are versatile: You can drift them downstream, retrieve them across stream, or jig them vertically.

DOWNSTREAM DRIFTING. To catch trout feeding in riffles, cast a $\frac{1}{32}$- to $\frac{1}{80}$-ounce (0.89 to 0.35 g) microjig upstream, then let it drift down through the riffle. Keep your rod tip high, reeling up slack as the jig drifts. Strikes may be hard to detect, but you can attach a strike indicator, just as you would in nymph fishing.

For casting these tiny jigs, use a $4\frac{1}{2}$- to $5\frac{1}{2}$-foot (1.4 to 1.7 m) ultralight spinning rod with a slow to medium action. Spool your reel with limp, 2- to 4-pound (0.9 to 1.8 kg) mono.

CROSS-STREAM RETRIEVE. In deeper water, use a heavier jig, $\frac{1}{16}$ to $\frac{1}{4}$ ounce (1.8 to 7.1 g). Quarter your cast upstream, aiming for targets like boulders and logs. Let the jig sink to the bottom, then retrieve it in a series of short twitches, lowering the jig back to the bottom with a taut line after each twitch. If the bottom-bouncing technique doesn't pay off, try a twitching retrieve in the mid-depths and just beneath the surface. Sometimes a faster retrieve will trigger a strike.

With these heavier jigs, use a medium-power, fast-action spinning rod, from $5\frac{1}{4}$ to 6 feet (1.6 to 1.8 m) in length, with limp 4- to 8-pound (1.8 to 3.6 kg) mono.

VERTICAL JIGGING. This technique works well for salmon and large trout in deep pools and runs of good-sized rivers. Simply lower a jig or jigging spoon to the bottom, then jig vertically as the boat drifts downstream. Keep your line taut as the lure sinks; set the hook at the slightest tug. Use a lure weighing from $\frac{3}{8}$ ounce to 2 ounces (10.6 to 56.7 g), depending on current speed and water depth.

A heavy baitcasting outfit works best for vertical jigging. Use a 5 $\frac{1}{2}$- to 6-foot (1.7 to 1.8 m), fast-action rod with 12- to 20-pound (5.5 to 9.1 kg) mono. For salmon, you may need mono up to 30-pound (13.6 kg) test.

CASTING WITH HARDWARE

The term "hardware" means all hard-bodied lures like spoons, spinners, and plugs. Hardware attracts trout by flash and vibration. By casting with hardware, you can cover a lot of water in a hurry. The technique works best from later spring through early fall, when higher water temperatures make trout more aggressive.

Compared to most other trout fishing techniques, hardware fishing is easy. Simply cast across stream, then regulate the speed of your retrieve so the lure ticks the bottom. When trout are actively feeding, ticking the bottom may not be necessary; the fish will swim upward to grab the lure.

Exactly how you angle your cast depends on the lure, the water depth, and the current speed. The more you angle it upstream, the deeper the lure will run. If the lure is bouncing on the bottom too much, angle the cast farther downstream. This way, water resistance from the current will keep the lure off the bottom.

Standard spinners and thin spoons are popular in small streams, where distance casting is not important.

Sonic spinners, which have a shaft that passes through the blade, are extremely popular in the West. The blade starts turning at the very low retrieve speed.

Weight-forward spinners and medium to thick spoons are a better choice in bigger rivers, or in those with deep water or fast current. These heavier lures can be cast much farther, and they run deeper.

Floating minnow plugs work well in small streams, but sinking minnow plugs and diving crankbaits are more effective in deeper current. With spinners, spoons, and sinking minnow plugs, the slower you retrieve, the deeper the lures will run. Floating minnow plugs and crankbaits run deepest with a medium to medium-fast retrieve.

For casting spinners, small spoons, and minnow plugs, use a 5- to 6-foot (1.5 to 1.8 m) light spinning outfit with 2- to 6-pound (0.9 to 2.7 kg) mono; for larger spoons and diving plugs, use a 5 ½- to 7-foot (1.7 to 2.1 m) medium-power spinning outfit with 6- to 8-pound (2.7 to 3.6 kg) mono.

Steelhead and salmon fishermen often use 8- to 9-foot (2.4 to 2.7 m) medium- to heavy-power spinning rods with 8- to 17-pound (3.6 to 7.7 kg) mono.

To avoid line twist, attach spinners and spoons with a small ball-bearing snap-swivel. Or, splice in a swivel about 6 inches (15.2 cm) ahead of the lure. Attach minnow plugs with a small snap or a Duncan loop knot; attach crankbaits with a snap or a double clinch knot.

Crank a floating minnow plug through a riffle in early morning or late evening to catch feeding trout. From a downstream position, cast to the head of the riffle, then reel rapidly through the riffle and the downstream run. After a few casts, move to the next riffle.

Hang your lure in the current to fish hard-to-reach pockets such as holes beneath log jams, brush piles, overhanging limbs, or undercut banks. From an upstream position, cast just short of the pocket, let out a little line, then allow the current to work your lure.

Work the cover farthest downstream and closest to you first. Then, a hooked fish will not spook others in unfished water when the current sweeps it downstream, or in unfished water close to you when you reel it in.

TROLLING

When you troll, your lure is in the water all the time, maximizing your chances of catching fish. Trolling offers several other advantages over casting: It's an easier technique for the novice; it enables you to cover more water; and where multiple lines are legal, you can troll with several lures at once.

Trolling works best in big rivers that have long stretches of deep water with slow to moderate current. It's not well-suited to river stretches with lots of riffles or rapids, and not recommended for shallow or very clear water. Because the boat passes over the fish before the lure arrives, spooking may be a big problem. You can reduce spooking by trolling in S-curves. This way the lure does not track continuously in the boat's wake.

Another way to avoid spooking fish is to troll with side planers (photo above). These devices attach to your line, pulling it well to the side of the boat's wake. They also let you cover a wider swath of water. Another way to fish side planers is to walk along shore, using the planer to carry your line to midstream waters you couldn't reach by casting.

Diving planes also attach to your line, taking the lure deep. The unweighted type is all you need in most streams; weighted ones generally run too deep.

You can troll for practically any salmonid, but the technique is used most often for anadromous fishes like steelhead and Pacific salmon.

Baitcasting gear works best for trolling. A good trolling rod is 7 to 9 feet (2.1 to 2.7 m) long, stiff enough to handle the water resistance against the lure, but light enough at the tip to telegraph the lure's action. Use abrasion-resistant mono, from 6- to 20-pound (2.7 to 9.1 kg) test depending on the size of the fish. A depth finder helps you follow breaks in the bottom contour.

Most anglers troll with deep-diving crankbaits. You can also use minnow plugs, spoons, jigs, and spinner-and-bait combinations. It's a good idea to keep your lures near the bottom, except when trout are feeding on insects or salmon smolts, and will come up for a lure. Pacific salmon and steelhead feed very little in streams, but may strike a deep-running crankbait out of irritation or in defense of their territory. Normally, no extra weight is needed to get a crankbait to the bottom, but you may have to add weight to other lures.

Trolling styles used in stream fishing for trout and salmon include slipping, upstream trolling, and downstream trolling.

SLIPPING. The term "slipping" means letting the boat drift slowly downstream, reducing its speed with a motor or oars while allowing the lures to trail in the current. As long as the boat drifts more slowly than the current, the force of the water will give the lures action. Some trout fishermen refer to this technique as "backtrolling."

To cover wide channels, zigzag your boat while slipping. This allows you to cover more water on the drift, a big adventure if you don't have a motor. It also gives your lures more action, causing them to speed up and slow down, rise and fall.

Slipping is effective year-round, but works especially well in cold water; the slow-moving lure appeals to lethargic fish. The technique has one major advantage over other trolling methods: The lure passes over the fish before the boat does, so they're less likely to spook.

UPSTREAM TROLLING. You can troll upstream only in slow current. Otherwise, water resistance is so great that the lure is forced to the surface. Where the current is slow enough you can troll upstream, then turn around and troll back down, keeping your lures in the water.

DOWNSTREAM TROLLING. This technique is often used to present spinners or other lures that do not require much current for good action. Trolling downstream slightly faster than the current gives these lures enough action, yet they look like drifting food. To troll slowly enough, you may have to shift your motor between forward and neutral every few seconds. When using lures like spoons and crankbaits, you will have to troll somewhat faster.

By trolling downstream, you are in a better position to fight the fish. The current pushes a hooked fish in the direction the boat moves, reducing the possibility of breaking the line or tearing out the hooks.

SPINFISHING WITH FLIES

Even if you don't own a fly rod, you can fly fish with spinning gear. In fact, spinning with flies works better than fly fishing in some situations. In deep water, for instance, you can attach split shot to mono line and reach bottom more easily than with fly line. Also, in high winds, mono is easier to control.

In streams with flies-only regulations, spinning gear is usually legal, as long as the lure is a fly. However, to cast the fly you must attach some extra weight.

With a sinking fly, simply add a split shot or two about a foot (30 cm) up the line. Leader wrap, lead sleeves, or a good-sized strike indicator will also add weight. Strike indicators help detect light pickups as well.

Dry flies and sinking flies can be rigged with a weighted float or a plastic bubble, which can be partially filled with water for extra casting weight. If you use a clear float or bubble, trout will pay little attention to it. Then again, a float or bubble splashing down close to a fish, or drifting over it ahead of the fly, may cause it to spook.

A long, soft rod is best for casting flies and manipulating them in the water. A stiff rod doesn't flex enough to cast a light weight, and could snap a light leader when you set the hook. A 6½- to 7½-foot (1.9 to 2.3 m), slow-action spinning rod, or an 8½- to 9½-foot (2.6 to 2.9 m), 4- to 6-weight fly rod with a spinning reel is a good choice. Spool your reel with 2- to 8-pound (0.9 to 3.6 kg), limp mono.

Many spinfishermen use line that is too heavy, and add too much weight, inhibiting the movement of the fly. Always use the lightest line practical for the conditions, and the lightest weight that will allow you to cast and reach the desired depth. Too much weight causes snagging problems; and even with minimal weight, strikes are more difficult to detect than with fly-fishing gear.

OTHER RIGS FOR SPINFISHING WITH FLIES

Make a dropper rig (top) by tying a blood knot 2 feet (0.6 m) up your line, leaving a 1-foot (0.3 m) tag end. Tie a float or bubble to the line, a dry fly or terrestrial to the dropper. Make a split shot rig (bottom) by pinching shot 6 to 12 inches (15.2 to 30.5 cm) above the fly.

HOW TO FISH A DROPPER RIG

Quarter your cast upstream above a rise, then raise your rod so the fly just reaches the water. Drift the fly over the rise, making sure you keep the float out of the fish's window. Occasionally lift the rod to dabble the fly on the surface.

TIPS FOR SPINFISHING WITH FLIES

Use a leader sleeve instead of split shot when fishing on a snaggy bottom. The cylindrical sleeve slips along the bottom better than a round split shot. Slide the sleeve onto your line, then tie on a leader; the knot acts as a stop.

Tie a wet-fly/dry-fly rig for use with a plastic bubble. Make a dropper by tying a blood knot, leaving a 3-inch (7.6 cm) tag end. Tie a dry fly to the dropper; it doubles as a strike indicator. Tie a wet fly to the end of the line.

NATURAL BAIT

Fly fishermen frown on the idea of using spoons, spinners, and other hardware to catch trout, and the idea of using natural bait is even farther down their list of tolerable tactics. Still, there's no denying that natural bait catches lots of trout, and it's often the method of choice for introducing children to the sport. If you wish to use natural bait, read the local fishing regulations carefully to make certain it's permitted on the waters you're fishing.

The major drawback of natural bait is the problem of deep hooking. Even a small trout often takes the bait so deeply that it's impossible to remove the hook without causing serious injury. If you plan to release your trout, don't use live bait. If you must release a deeply hooked trout, cut the line rather than trying to remove the hook.

Another disadvantage of many natural baits is the difficulty of keeping them alive and carrying them, especially if you're wading. Also, in some states, certain natural baits, like minnows, are illegal for trout.

Trout and salmon rely on their sense of smell to a greater extent than most other gamefish. They can detect dissolved substances in minute concentrations, as evidenced by the ability of sea-run salmon and steelhead to return to their home stream on the basis of its unique odor. So it's not surprising that they use their remarkable sense of smell to help them find food.

Natural bait appeals to this highly developed sense. Smell is especially important during periods of high, muddy water. Under these conditions, trout cannot see flies or hardware, but they can easily detect the odor of natural bait.

In early spring, when the water is still cold and few insects are hatching, natural bait usually outproduces flies by a wide margin. Natural bait is also a good choice in streams that do not have many insects. In addition, big trout or those in heavily fished streams can be extremely wary, closely inspecting any potential food item. They're likely to recognize any imitation as a fake.

Push a size 6 or 8 hook through the broken end of a half crawler (top), or through the middle whole crawler (bottom) Or, hook the crawler two or three times, like a garden worm.

Bait fishermen often make the mistake of using heavy line and a big hook, then adding a heavy sinker and a golf ball-sized bobber. This type of rig will seldom catch a trout. For most stream trout, bait-fishing specialists use light spinning tackle with 2- to 4-pound (0.9 to 1.8 kg) mono, size 6 to 12 hooks, and a split shot for weight. Of course large trout and salmon require heavier tackle, but seldom will you need line heavier than 8-pound (3.6 kg) test or a hook larger than size 2.

The variety of trout and salmon baits is nearly endless. Garden worms, night crawlers, and salmon eggs are the most common baits, along with minnows and cut fish. Leeches, adult and larval insects, and crayfish are not as popular, but are no less effective. Fishermen have also discovered that certain "grocery baits," like marshmallows and corn, work extremely well, especially for stocked trout.

Although most trout will take any of these baits, some have a distinct preference. Also, a given bait may be more productive at certain times of year or under certain water conditions.

Fishermen have discovered that wax worms (bee moth larvae) and other larval baits used for ice fishing are excellent for trout. They work particularly well in winter, when most other baits are hard to find. Their small size is an advantage when the water is cold and trout feeding slows.

DRIFT FISHING

Drift fishing accounts for more trout and salmon than any other bait-fishing technique. The idea is to present your bait so it drifts naturally with the current, just like real food.

You can drift fish for everything from small brookies to trophy steelhead and salmon. The basic technique is the same, only the gear is different.

Position yourself to the side and just downstream of a riffle or run likely to hold trout. Most pools do not have enough current to keep your bait drifting. Before casting, look for boulders, logs, or other likely cover, then quarter your cast upstream so the bait will skirt the object as it drifts.

Light spinning gear works best for average-sized trout. A 6- to 7-foot (1.8 to 2.1 m) medium-action rod is long enough for good line control, yet flexible enough for lobbing delicate baits. The lighter the line you use, the easier it is to achieve a drag-free drift. Heavy line has more water resistance, so the current creates a larger belly and the bait begins to drift too fast. Limp, clear, 4-pound (1.8 kg) mono is a good all-around choice, but you may need heavier line if the bottom is snaggy.

Some drift fishermen use a fly rod with a spinning reel. The longer rod gives them even better line control and makes it easier to dunk the bait into hard-to-reach spots.

Steelhead and salmon anglers commonly use 8- to 10-weight fly rods, and fly reels loaded with 8- to 17-pound (3.6 to 7.7 kg) abrasion-resistant mono. With a rod this long, you can drift your bait, usually a spawn bag or some type of spawn imitation, through narrow runs with perfect control. Simply swing the bait upstream, walk it through the run, then swing it upstream again. This repetitious presentation is the best way to entice a strike from fish that aren't really feeding.

In drift fishing, it's important to select a sinker of the proper weight. Too heavy, and it will hang on the bottom so the bait cannot drift as fast as the current. Too light, and the current will lift the bait off the bottom. You must choose a sinker heavy enough so that it just ticks the bottom as the bait drifts. Carry a selection of sinkers and split shot in various sizes, and use different ones to suit the conditions.

Almost any natural bait tough enough to stay on the hook will work for drift fishing. A delicate bait like an adult mayfly would probably tear off. You can add visual appeal by snelling a small piece of fluorescent yarn on your hook just ahead of the bait. In fact, many steelhead and salmon anglers use only the yarn.

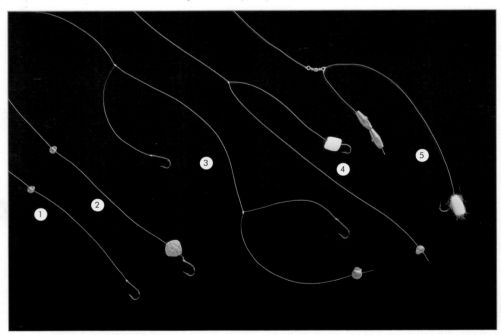

Drift-Fishing Rigs include: (1) Basic split shot rig; (2) Split shot rig with drift bobber for extra attraction and for keeping bait off bottom; (3) Double-dropper rig for fishing with two baits. The split shot pulls off when snagged; (4) Marshmallow rig for floating bait off bottom; and (5) Drift-sinker rig with yarn fly.

PLUNKING

Practically every experienced trout fisherman has been badly outfished at some time or other by a kid plunking worms into a pool. While the technique is not glamorous, it accounts for plenty of trout.

The term plunking simply means still-fishing. The usual technique is to attach a sinker to the line, bait up, lob a cast into a pool, then sit back and wait.

Plunking works especially well for big trout. If you sit quietly, they eventually detect the scent and swim over to investigate. If you continually cast and retrieve the bait, you are likely to spook them.

Almost any live bait will work, but night crawlers and minnows are most popular. In stocked streams, anglers often plunk with Velveeta cheese and other junk food. Browns, rainbows, and cutthroat seem most susceptible to plunking.

Use only enough weight to keep your bait from drifting. If you attach a heavy sinker, the fish will feel resistance and spit the bait. In small streams, a split shot is normally adequate, but in bigger streams, you may need a small slip sinker. Most anglers plunk with light spinning gear and 4- to 8-pound (1.8 to 3.6 kg) mono, depending on the size of the trout and the snagginess of the bottom.

PLUNKING TIPS

Make an easy-to-tie slip-sinker rig by threading an egg sinker onto the line, pinching on a small split shot about 2 feet (0.6 m) up the line, then attaching a hook.

Float your bait off the bottom by threading on a small marshmallow so it rides just ahead of the hook. Or, hook your bait on a floating jig head.

Chapter 6
TECHNIQUES FOR SPECIAL SITUATIONS

Woody Allen once said, "Eighty percent of success is just showing up." The same can be said of trout fishing. The reality is that not every day on the water is going to be perfect. Heavy rains, drought, heavy cover, darkness, and the long winter season, can all conspire to keep the fair-weather fisherman off the water. But the angler who knows how to handle these situations can extend his or her season and greatly increase their chances of success.

Of course, you should always check the regulations wherever you are planning to fish to ensure that it's legal to fish after dark, for example, or whether there is a winter trout-fishing season. In some states and provinces, prolonged drought can prompt fisheries managers to close rivers or regions to avoid excessive pressure on stressed fish, and high water can be particularly dangerous to the ill-prepared angler. But once you've determined the regulations, you can turn these special situations to your advantage.

The following pages will show you how to change up your approach, choose the proper gear, modify your casting style, or switch your fly and lure selection to adapt to whatever tricky conditions you may encounter. In fact, once you understand how to approach special situations, such as winter season or night fishing, you may find yourself reaching for your fishing gear when other fishermen are at home, giving you that most-cherished situation of all: a river to yourself.

HIGH WATER

To trout fishermen, high water can be a blessing or a curse. Runoff from a heavy rain or rapid snowmelt raises the stream level and discolors the water, but the effects of these changes depend upon the type of stream and your method of fishing.

Rising water draws anadromous trout and salmon into streams. Fishing may be tough as long as the water stays muddy, but as it starts to clear, the action picks up dramatically. Fishing peaks when the water is clearing, but still somewhat discolored.

Spin fishermen can get their lures deep simply by using more weight, but it's not as easy for fly fishermen. Split shot, lead-core line, shooting heads, and large weighted nymphs and streamers all help to solve the problem. However, trout still will have difficulty spotting a fly.

Flies and lures that produce vibration are more effective in discolored water. Trout detect the vibrations with their lateral-line sense. Bright colors also help. Fly materials like Flashabou, Krystal Flash, and tinsel improve the visibility of streamers and large wet flies. In extremely muddy water, natural bait—where allowed—can be most effective. Trout can smell the bait, even when they can't see it.

Streams vary in the amount of time necessary for the water to clear and return to normal level. It may take two weeks in a stream with a large drainage area, but only a few hours in one with a small drainage. In tailwater streams, the water may rise and fall daily.

Generally, headwaters clear first. If the lower reaches of a stream are too muddy for fly fishing, you may find water that's clear enough by moving upstream. Sometimes you only have to go far enough to get above a muddy tributary.

LOW WATER

When the water is low and the stream shrinks to a fraction of its former size, all the trout concentrate in a few key spots, usually the deepest pools, runs, and undercuts. Consequently, you can find the trout much more easily than in high water. But low water also means clear water, so the fish are spookier and more selective.

With the water so transparent, it's easier to walk along the stream and spot the trout, but they can also see you more clearly. The low water leaves them fewer places to hide, and thus more visible to predators, so the trout become much warier.

When trout become super-selective, fly fishermen gain an edge over anglers using other methods. Not only does a fly have a natural look, but it also allows a presentation more delicate than possible with other lures and baits. In low, clear water, fly fishermen use rods of 5-weight or lighter, leaders as long as 15 feet (4.6 m), and tippets as light as 7X.

Flies for low water are smaller than normal, usually size 16 or under, with drab, natural colors. Dries and nymphs generally work better than streamers. Terrestrial patterns, like a black ant, are a good choice when nothing is rising. Low-water periods usually correspond to the times when terrestrial insects are most numerous.

How you approach trout is even more important when the water is low and clear. Under these conditions, step lightly, keep a low profile, wear drab clothing and avoid throwing a shadow across the stream.

Low-water fishing is usually best in overcast or windy weather; trout cannot see you as well as they could under calm, sunny conditions. Trout are most active in early morning, around dusk, or at night. In midday, they tuck into heavy cover or move to deep water and feed very little.

HEAVY COVER

If you were to watch fisheries workers electrofishing a small trout stream, you'd be amazed at the number of trout living in dense brush piles, weed beds, and log jams, or far beneath undercut banks and overhanging limbs.

Stream trout are conditioned to seek heavy cover at an early age. Soon after they emerge from the redd, they face attacks from predatory insects, birds, and fish, including larger trout. Those that learn to find the cover that affords the greatest protection have the best chance of survival.

Many anglers do not even attempt to fish these prime spots, for fear of getting snagged. You can't escape the fact that snags will be a problem, but if you want to catch these wary trout, which usually are the biggest trout, you must learn to fish heavy cover.

By learning to side cast with a fly rod, for instance, you can place a fly beneath overhanging branches. A side cast is just like a conventional cast, except that you hold the rod parallel to the water. With a little practice you can cast beneath cover only a few inches off the water, precisely controlling your distance.

Fly fishing also works well for fishing undercut banks. You can often drift a fly beneath a bank that could not be reached with other lures or bait.

Trout tucked into dense weed beds are difficult to catch on spinning lures because weeds quickly foul the hooks. However, you can easily float a dry fly over the weed tops, or fish a sinking fly in pockets or channels in the weeds. With fly tackle you can cast across a weed bed to open water, retrieve the fly to the edge of the weeds, then pick it up for another cast without dragging it back through them.

Jigs work well for drawing trout out of heavy cover. Cast as close to a log jam, brush pile, or undercut as you can; a jig sinks fast enough to reach the fish zone before the current carries it away.

You can also draw trout from heavy cover with a spinner or small spoon. Position yourself upstream, cast down to the cover, then hang the lure in the current along the upstream edge and sides.

When you hook a trout, try to get it away from the cover immediately. If you let it run, it will invariably head for the thickest tangle of weeds or brush.

With any of these heavy-cover techniques, it pays to use heavier-than-normal line and tippets, preferably abrasion-resistant mono. Soft mono scuffs too easily and could cost you a good trout.

HOW TO FLY FISH AN UNDERCUT

Allow the fly to drift freely; if the current is angling into the bank, it will pull the fly beneath the overhang where trout can easily see it.

TIPS FOR FISHING HEAVY COVER

Flick a sidearm cast under overhanging brush. Raise the rod slightly on the back cast so the line won't slap the water behind you; lower it as the line unrolls to the rear, then make a forward cast just above the water.

Unsnag a fly by raising your rod tip, then throwing a loop as if making a roll cast. When the loop unrolls on the opposite side of the snag, the fly will usually pull free.

NIGHT FISHING

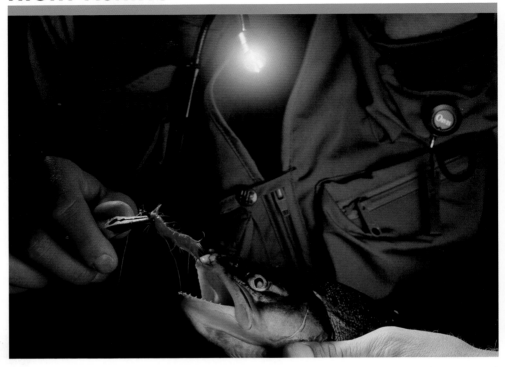

To many, the notion of fishing a trout stream at night evokes thoughts of tripping over logs and tangling lines in streamside brush. To others, night fishing means big trout, especially browns.

Big browns stay in heavy cover during daylight hours, but at night they seem to lose their caution. They feed in shallow riffles and tails of pools, often far from cover, and are not nearly as selective as in daylight. Cutthroat and rainbows also feed at night, but to a lesser extent.

Night fishing is most effective during low-water periods in summer, when the clarity increases because of the low flow, and the water temperature rises into the 70s (21°C). At night the water may cool to the mid-60s (17 to 18°C), a more likely temperature for feeding, and the clarity is actually an advantage. Moonless, starry nights are best; trout are less wary in the dark of the moon, but the stars provide enough light so you can see a little.

Before attempting to fish at night, scout the water during the day. Make note of likely trout lies, overhead branches, or other obstacles that could

Doctor plugs, spinners, and spoons with luminescent tape to improve lure visibility when night fishing. But do not use tape that glows too brightly; it will spook the fish. You can also buy luminescent fly-tying materials.

foul your cast, and deep holes that mean you could easily land a good-sized trout. Nighttime is not the time to check out new water.

Fly fishermen most commonly use streamers, nymphs, or leech imitations, usually in large sizes. During a major hatch, you can often hear trout rising. In this situation, dry flies can be very effective. Many night fishermen prefer big, heavily hackled dry flies because they are easier to see, and produce plenty of vibrations so trout can quickly locate them. A light-colored fly is also easier to see, and at night the exact color is not as important as the silhouette.

Because the fish are more aggressive at night, your presentation need not be as delicate as in daylight. In fact, a fly splatting down on the water may actually attract a trout's attention. You can get by with a 6- to 8-pound (2.7 to 3.6 kg) spinning line or fly tippet, so if you do get snagged in streamside brush you can pull loose.

You don't need a lot of special equipment for night fishing, but unless you're very familiar with the streambed, it's a good idea to wear waders instead of hip boots. Bug spray, a flashlight, and a light that attaches to your vest also come in handy.

TIPS FOR NIGHT FISHING

Attach your fly with a tiny metal clip. This way, you do not have to tie knots in the dark.

Spool on white fly line for night fishing. Any light-colored line will be visible, but white shows up best.

WINTER FISHING

If you dislike crowds, try fishing your favorite trout stream in winter. Chances are you'll have the whole stream to yourself, and the trout can be surprisingly cooperative.

Of course, you should check the fishing regulations to make sure the stream is open. Many streams close before the fall spawning season and don't reopen until spring, and those that remain open often have special regulations, such as artificials-only and catch-and-release.

Most winter fishing is for browns, rainbows, cutthroat, and brook trout, but anglers on Pacific coast streams catch good numbers of winter-run steelhead. These fish enter the streams in late fall in preparation for spring spawning.

Trout behave much differently in near-freezing water than at summertime temperatures. Look for them in slower water and heavier cover. In most cases they're right on the bottom, although they will rise to feed on tiny emerging midges, or snowflies. Bright sunlight triggers these midge hatches, prompting trout to start feeding. Fly fishing with midge pupa patterns in sizes 18 to 28 can be very effective, especially on warm, sunny afternoons.

Many anglers think that flies this small must be difficult to use, so they shy away from midge fishing. But you can fish midges much the same way you fish nymphs, only with lighter gear. Most midge fishermen use a 2- to 4-weight fly rod from 8 to 9 feet (2.4 to 2.7 m) long. Midges work best when fished just beneath the surface film, so a floating, weight-forward fly line is a good choice. Use a 9- to 12-foot (2.7 to 3.7 m) tapered leader with a 6X to 8X tippet. Strikes on midges are often very subtle, so it pays to attach a sensitive strike indicator.

Dry flies are seldom used in winter, but streamers, nymphs, and scud patterns account for a fair number of trout. Streamers should be worked deep and slow. Nymphs and scuds should be dead-drifted, just as in summer.

As a rule, the best winter trout fishing is where the stream is warmest. Trout often congregate around springs because the ground water is normally warmer than the surrounding water. In some tailwater streams, trout stay near the dam because water discharged from the depths of the upstream reservoir is a few degrees warmer than water farther downstream.

TIPS FOR FISHING A MIDGE

Check snowy stream banks to determine if there is a midge hatch. Tiny dark insects resembling mosquitoes are probably midges; select a fly that resembles them.

Dead drift a midge imitation just beneath the surface film, rather than on the surface. Your tippet will be less visible and the sunken fly seems to have more appeal.

RESOURCES

Alaska Department of Fish and Wildlife
907 465 6085
www.adfg.state.ak.us

British Columbia Tourism
http://bcadventure.com

British Columbia Fish and Wildlife Branch
250 387 9771
www.env.gov.bc.ca/fw/

Fairbanks Convention and Visitors Bureau
www.explorefairbanks.com

Fishing Central Oregon
www.fishingcentraloregon.com
www.garylewisoutdoors.com

Fishing Southern Oregon
www.visitmedford.org
www.travelklamath.com

Fishing Tri-Cities Washington
www.www.visittri-cities.com

Freshwater Fisheries Society of BC
888 601 4200
www.gofishbc.com

Oregon Department of Fish and Wildlife
800 720 6339
www.dfw.state.or.us

Northwest Lunker
www.nwlunker.com

NorthwestTrout.com
editor@northwesttrout.com
www.northwesttrout.com

Pacific Northwest Fisheries Program
USDA Forest Service
www.fs.fed.us

Washington Department of Fish and Wildlife
360 902 2200
http://wdfw.wa.gov

Wild Fish Conservancy
425 788 1167
http://wildfishconservancy.org

PHOTO CREDITS

p. 4 photo © istock / www.istock.com

p. 6 photo © istock / www.istock.com

p. 7 photos © (top & lower) Gary Lewis

p. 8 photo © Fotosearch / SuperStock (Crater Lake, Oregon), www.fotosearch.com

p. 9 photos © Gary Lewis

p. 10 photo © Gary Lewis

p. 12 photo © Fotosearch/Corbis (Boathouses on Upper Klamath Lake), www.fotosearch.com

p. 13 photo © Gary Lewis

p. 14 photo © Fotosearch/Design Pics (Takhlakh Lake, Mount Adams), www.fotosearch.com

p. 15 photo © istock / www.istock.com

p. 17 photo © istock / www.istock.com

p. 19 photo © Miles Schmidt

p. 20 photo © (all) Miles Schmidt, www. MineralLake.com

p. 21 photo © Andrew Penner, istock / www.istock.com

p. 22 photo © Fotosearch / SuperStock (Chilcotin Mountains, British Columbia)

p. 23 photo © istock / www.istock.com

p. 24 photo © Fotosearch / Design Pics (Bugaboos Provincial Park, British Columbia)

p. 25 photo © Fotosearch / Design Pics (Meadow, Elk Lakes Provincial Park, British Columbia)

p. 26 photo © Fotosearch / Design Pics (Floe Lake, Kootenay National Park)

p. 27 photo © istock / www.istock.com

p. 28 to 30 and 31 (top) photos © Al Noraker

p. 31 (lower) photo © Gary Lewis

INDEX

Hunting Books
* Advanced Turkey Hunting
* Advanced Whitetail Hunting
* Beginner's Guide to Birdwatching
* Black Bear Hunting
* Bowhunting Equipment & Skills
* Bowhunter's Guide to Accurate Shooting
* The Complete Guide to Hunting
* Dog Training
* Elk Hunting
* How to Think Like a Survivor
* Hunting Record-Book Bucks
* Mule Deer Hunting
* Muzzleloading
* Outdoor Guide to Using Your GPS
* Waterfowl Hunting
* Whitetail Addicts Manual
* Whitetail Hunting
* Whitetail Techniques & Tactics
* Wild Turkey

Fishing Books
* Advanced Bass Fishing
* The Art of Freshwater Fishing
* The Complete Guide to Freshwater Fishing
* Fishing for Catfish
* Fishing Tips & Tricks
* Fishing with Artificial Lures
* Inshore Salt Water Fishing
* Kids Gone Campin'
* Kids Gone Fishin'
* Kids Gone Paddlin'
* Largemouth Bass
* Live Bait Fishing
* Modern Methods of Ice Fishing
* Northern Pike & Muskie
* Panfish
* Salt Water Fishing Tactics
* Smallmouth Bass
* Striped Bass Fishing: Salt Water Strategies
* Successful Walleye Fishing
* Ultralight Fishing

Fly Fishing Books
* The Art of Fly Tying + CD-ROM
* Complete Photo Guide to Fly Fishing
* Complete Photo Guide to Fly Tying
* Fishing Dry Flies
* Fly-Fishing Equipment & Skills
* Fly Fishing for Beginners
* Fly Fishing for Trout in Streams
* Fly-Tying Techniques & Patterns

Cookbooks
* All-Time Favorite Game Bird Recipes
* America's Favorite Fish Recipes
* America's Favorite Wild Game Recipes
* Backyard Grilling
* Cooking Wild in Kate's Kitchen
* Dressing & Cooking Wild Game
* The New Cleaning & Cooking Fish
* Preparing Fish & Wild Game
* The Saltwater Cookbook
* Venison Cookery
* The Wild Butcher
* The Wild Fish Cookbook
* The Wild Game Cookbook

To purchase these or other Creative Publishing international titles, contact your local bookseller, or visit our website at
www.creativepub.com

The Complete
FLY FISHERMAN™